THE YOUNGEST PROPHET

THE YOUNGEST PROPHET

The Life of Jacinta Marto, Fatima Visionary

by

Christopher Rengers, O.F.M. Cap.

ALBA · HOUSE NEW · YORK

SOCIETY OF ST. PAUL, 2187 VICTORY BLVD., STATEN ISLAND, NEW YORK 10314

ST PAULS

Library of Congress Cataloging-in-Publication Data

Rengers, Christopher.
  The youngest prophet.

   1. Marto, Jacinta, 1910-1920.   2. Blessed—
   Portugal—Biography.   3. Fatima, Our Lady of.
   I. Title.
   BX4705.M4134R46   1986
   282'.092'4 [B]   85-30789
   ISBN 0-8189-0496-8

Imprimi Potest:
Very Rev. Robert L. McCreary, OFM, Cap.
Provincial
Province of St. Augustine
January 2, 1986

Photos courtesy of the author and of *Soul* magazine.

Produced and designed in the United States of America by the
Fathers and Brothers of the Society of St. Paul,
2187 Victory Boulevard, Staten Island, New York 10314-6603,
as part of their communications apostolate.

ISBN: 0-8189-0496-8

Printing Information:

Current Printing - first digit		4	5	6	7	8	9	10

Year of Current Printing - first year shown

		2002	2003	2004	2005	2006	2007	2008	2009

Dedication

In gratitude

> To the memory of my parents, Bernard T. Rengers and Elizabeth A. *nee* Thinnes. They taught my brother Gerard and me to "offer it up" for the Poor Souls in Purgatory and for Poor Sinners.

Acknowledgments

For inspiration

Armand Dasseville, O.F.M. Cap. *Monthly Message*
St. John The Baptist, 210 W. 31st St., NY 10001
All-Night Vigil Group of D.C. 1320 Monroe St., N.E.
Washington, D.C. 20017

Fr. Armand's *Monthly Message* for his All-Night Vigilers in New York is reprinted by Virginia Murphy, organizer of the Washington group that keeps vigil every First Friday at St. Anthony Church in Washington, D.C. 9:00 p.m. to 6:00 a.m. Having either attended or taken part in the Washington vigils for ten years has been a great blessing. The devotedness of the people, their piety and good cheer are inspirational.

Milton Lomask and Fr. Sebastian Miklas, O.F.M. Cap.

The classes in *How To Write*, given at Catholic University under the Adult-Ed Office, 1975-76 by Mr. Lomask, led me to write an essay on Jacinta. Fr. Sebastian who administered the Adult-Ed encouraged me to take the classes. The essay in due course grew into a book.

For help

Mr. and Mrs. Thomas McCafferty of South Croydon, Surrey, England, for typing and promotional work. A three-part series, adapted from the text of *The Youngest Prophet*, was published in the *Scottish Catholic Observer* due to their help.

Mrs. Sandra Regina, Mrs. Pietra Giganti, Mrs. Thomy Guida for typing; Bob Nesnick of Fatima, Portugal for printed cards and photos, and the inspiration of his life given full time to St. Therese, Jacinta and Francisco.

Always and everywhere to good St. Joseph.

A Special Note of Thanks to His Excellency, Most Rev. Sean O'Malley, Bishop of the Virgin Islands. As. Fr. Sean, O.F.M. Cap. he was for many years a confrere at Capuchin College, Wash. D.C. During this time he worked in and directed the Hispanic and Social Development Apostolates in the Archdiocese. His doctoral studies at Catholic University were in the areas of Spanish literature and mysticism.

Table of Contents

(Photo section between pages 80-81)

Jacinta the Prophet

On February 20, 1920, a little girl named Jacinta Marto died after a long illness. She was less than a month away from her tenth birthday. In the ordinary course of events, this little girl would never have come to the attention of the world at large. She would have been remembered only by her family and friends.

But Jacinta was no ordinary little girl. Besides being one of the three Fatima seers, her brief life had such a quality of holiness and prophetic witness that since December 20, 1979, she has been an approved candidate for beatification. If she and her brother Francisco (whose separate process is at the same stage) are eventually canonized, they will be the youngest non-martyrs ever to receive that honor.

The first seven years of Jacinta's life were uneventful, spent with her parents Manuel and Olympia Marto in Aljustrel, a town near Fatima in Portugal. But in 1917, Jacinta, her brother Francisco, and their cousin Lucia dos Santos had a series of remarkable experiences which brought them to world attention. Between May-October 1917, they had a series of visions of Our Lady, which will be fully described in the main body of this book. At the time, Jacinta was 7, Francisco was 9, and Lucia was 10 years old.

On September 7, 1917, a young attorney named Dr. Carlos Mendes visited the three children in Aljustrel who by this time were attracting attention all over Portugal. The next day, he wrote to his fiancee:

When I arrived at Aljustrel, at the house of Francisco's parents, I asked to speak to the children. Jacinta appeared and came to me at once. She is very tiny, very babyish ... I must tell you at once that she is a darling—a little angel. She had a red handkerchief on her head, the points tied behind . . . the handkerchief served to emphasize her features. Her eyes are very dark and enchantingly vivacious, while her expression is really angelic, so extraordinarily sweet and kind that one is attracted in spite of oneself. She was so shy and timid... Francisco arrived ... He has a splendid boyish face, and his expression is both lively and manly ... Jacinta began to gain courage. Shortly afterwards Lucia arrived. You cannot imagine Jacinta's joy when she saw her! She seemed to dissolve into laughter, and ran to her cousin, never leaving her side again.

Lucia is not very impressive to look at ... her expression is lively, but for the rest she is ordinary looking . . . All three children say that a Lady appeared to them, but they do not know who she is. On the 13th of October she will say who she is and what she wants. The naturalness and simplicity with which they tell one all this is extraordinary and impressive. Lucia sees the Lady, speaks to her and hears her. Jacinta sees and hears her, but does not address her. Francisco neither hears nor speaks, but sees her. The difference is very interesting, is it not? . . .

It is now my conviction that we are confronted with something outside mere reason. I await October 13th with growing impatience . . . The chief impression of the children seems to be of the Lady's beauty . . . I showed Francisco your photograph and asked him if she were prettier than you. "Much more," he said, "and the Lady was all dressed in white and gold."

On October 13, some 70,000 people gathered in the rain on the Cova da Iria. At noon solar time, the three children again saw the Lady. The crowd did not see her, but shortly witnessed an amazing sign. Dr. Domingos Pinto Coelho, an eminent eye specialist, reported what happened in the newspaper, *A Ordem*:

> The sun, at one moment surrounded with scarlet flame, at another aureoled in yellow and deep purple, seemed to be in an exceedingly fast and whirling movement, at times appearing to be loosened from the sky and to be approaching the earth, strongly radiating heat.

This lasted about 12 minutes. Many in the crowd cried out in terror. Some knelt to beg God's forgiveness. The people and their clothing, soaked by the long downpour of rain, suddenly were dry.

That evening, October 13, at 7 P.M., Fr. Manuel Formigao, a seminary professor from Santarem, questioned the three children separately (see Appendix A). One of Lucia's answers summed up the message they had received from Our Lady: "She said we were to amend our lives and not offend the Lord anymore because He was too much offended already, and that we were to say the rosary and ask pardon for our sins."

Over the years, the Church has studied the events at Fatima, and has approved them as much as a private revelation can be approved. Pius XII, Paul VI and John Paul II stand out as strong devotees of the Fatima message.

Most accounts of Fatima have centered on Lucia. This was inevitable: she is still alive at the time of writing (1986) as a Carmelite nun in Coimbra, and many details of the Fatima message (and accounts of later private revelations) come from her alone. Jacinta died in 1920 and Francisco in 1919.

Being the recipient of a private revelation does not automatically mean that a person has the heroic sanctity required of a canonized saint. Bernadette Soubirous, the Lourdes seer, was canonized; Melanie Calvat and Maximin Giraud, the La Salette seers, were not.

Jacinta was not simply a seer; she was a prophet as well. In her, we see love for God and for others developed to an heroic degree. She is a delightful model and guide. Of the three children, she was the tenderest of heart and years. She accepted the message of the vision and carried out its requests with complete generosity. She is the youngest prophet.

What is a prophet? It is a person who has a message for the present. Predictions of the future, heavenly voices, beautiful visions or unusual dreams are not the main issue. The important thing is the voice of the authentic prophet telling us of God's plans, of how His justice and mercy work out, depending on the cooperation or non-cooperation of many people whose names will never be in the history books or in the news.

When Jonah went to Nineveh and proclaimed that God would destroy the city, the chief point was that, here and now, the Ninevites should repent and humble themselves before God by prayer and fasting. They did so, from the king to the least of his subjects, and the city was spared.

Although Jonah's prediction had been made in absolute terms, its fulfillment depended on whether or not the people repented. So it was with the predictions of the Old Testament prophets—Isaiah, Ezekiel, Jeremiah, etc. We usually think of a prophet as one who foretells the future. This is because a prophet often gives a warning about the future, telling what will happen *if* people do not repent.

God's communications do not have to be extraordinary. A prophet is also one to whom God gives special insight into the present. Such a prophet has a quiet gift—the flowing of the Holy Spirit into his own convictions. He shows people the path God wants them to take, by traveling on it himself. The prophet holds a God-given light showing us the path on which God wants us to take the first step. Sometimes the beam shows us something lying far ahead. But our real need is for light to show us where to take the next step.

Throughout history, God has favored us with prophets. What some of them said is incorporated in Holy Scripture. The time of public, scriptural revelation is ended, but God continues to send special spokesmen or prophets. At bottom, the message of Fatima is the same as the message of the Old Testament prophets: Amend your life, pray and make sacrifices. Wars are the punishment for sins.

Being a prophet is not easy. Many of the Old Testament prophets were killed. True prophets are revealed by their manner of life and their willingness to become martyrs. John the Baptist's way of life gave credence to his preaching. His martyrdom for the sake of truth showed that he passed the final test of a true prophet.

Prophets must be generous and courageous. They do not have an easy time. They possess a message, but the message also possesses them. Jesus in His humanity was the greatest prophet. He told us that no man is a prophet in his own town. His neighbors were ready to throw Him over a cliff. Eventually, His proclamation of God's message led Him to Calvary.

We have to distinguish between true and false prophets, and we also must subject the true prophet to close scrutiny.

The prophet does not have an infallible pipeline from heaven. Everything he says is not necessarily an authentic part of the message God gave him. Everything the prophet later advises or upholds is not necessarily based on correct judgment. The Catholic Church uses the revealed truths of faith together with the cold, clear light of reason to evaluate what a prophet proclaims from a private revelation. We cannot uncritically accept everything a true prophet says. Neither, on the other hand, can we dismiss their entire message through excessive skepticism.

At Fatima, in the final analysis, we do not have the words of Mary but the words of the children who reported what she said to them. Francisco did not hear Mary; only Jacinta and Lucia had that privilege.

Jacinta is a child of the twentieth century who repeats an ancient scriptural truth: pray and do penance. She repeats it in a new way and with new particulars. Maybe the particulars aren't intended for everybody, but the essentials of the message are.

Peace is everybody's business. Jacinta, youngest of the prophets, spoke and lived out a plan that leads to peace. Her words and her life cast a clear beam of light on the path God wants many to follow. If enough follow this path with enough generosity, their prayers and sacrifices will raise a protective umbrella over the world which no nuclear bomb can pierce.

The Life of Jacinta Marto, Fatima Visionary

Chapter One

The Little Shepherdess

Between 1935 and 1941, Lucia wrote four Memoirs about Fatima at the order of her bishop. These Memoirs have been translated into English as the book *Fatima In Lucia's Own Words*. Besides being a basic source of information about Fatima, they could well become a spiritual classic like St. Therese's *Story Of A Soul*.

The first Memoir concentrated on Jacinta, and the other Memoirs gave additional information about her. They are vital for an understanding of Jacinta's holy life and message. We will be freely drawing on them in the following pages.

Lucia begins her first Memoir in a matter-of-fact way that highlights the unpleasant side of Jacinta's very sensitive soul:

"Before the events of 1917, except for the ties of kinship, no particular affection led me to prefer Jacinta's and Francisco's companionship to that of any other child. On the contrary, her companionship sometimes became too unpleasant because her character was so susceptible. The slightest conflict, which usually arises among children when they are playing, was enough to make her sulk in a corner—'fastening the little donkey' as we used to say. The sweetest caresses the children used to give on such occasions were not enough to make her come back to play. It was necessary to let her choose the game and the partner she liked to play with."

Lucia was the story-teller, the outgoing child, a leader among the children of the little hamlet of Aljustrel. Francisco and Jacinta did not mix that easily and preferred Lucia's company and sought her out. Besides wanting to choose the games, Jacinta had another defect. Sometimes she wanted to keep the prizes, although these were not "for keeps." Olympia Marto and Maria Rosa dos Santos in some ways were quite indulgent mothers. One game involved the snipping off of buttons from clothing. The buttons had to be re-sewn. But if Jacinta had had her way, Lucia would not even have had the buttons to take home with her.

But Lucia concludes, "She was good at heart, and God had endowed her with a sweet and tender character which made her, at the same time, amiable and attractive."

Jacinta's mother, Olympia, said with a touch of pride about footwear, "She liked to have her hair tidy, and I used to do it for her every day. A little jacket and a cotton skirt and shoes were what she wore each day, for I was always able to keep my children shod."

Jacinta's father, Manuel, usually called Ti (Uncle) Marto, was not a man given to favorites or exaggerated expression. He says of Jacinta:

"She was always gentle and sweet, and she was like that from the beginning. If she wanted anything, she would let us know in her own way, or just give a tiny cry, and then no more trouble at all. When we went out to Mass, or for some other reason left the house, she did not mind. We never had to go through any nonsense because of her. She was naturally good and was the sweetest among our children."

At the beginning of the fourth Memoir Lucia draws a comparison between Francisco and Jacinta. "Francisco didn't seem to be the brother of Jacinta other than in facial

features and in the practice of virtue. He was not like her—
capricious and vivacious. On the contrary, he had a pacific
and complaisant temperament." Jacinta wanted her own
way at games. Francisco did not even defend his rights. He
would say, "Do you think you won? That's all right. I don't
care." He was so nonchalant that it irritated Lucia at times.
She felt that if Francisco had grown to manhood, his chief
defect would be, "Don't bother about it." "He was not like
Jacinta fond of dance, but preferred to play his fife while the
other children were dancing . . . They used to wait for me at
my parents' courtyard, and while Jacinta ran to meet me as
soon as she heard the bells of the flock, he waited, sitting on
the stone steps at the front door . . ."

Jacinta preferred the moonlight to the sunlight. She
called the sun, the Lamp of Our Lord, and the moon, the
Lamp of Our Lady. Francisco differed. "No Lamp is as
beautiful as that of Our Lord," he said to Jacinta. She preferred the Lamp of Our Lady because it didn't hurt her eyes.
Jacinta called the stars Angels' Lanterns. Sometimes she and
Francisco tried to count them. Lucia offers an explanation
for Jacinta's preference for the moonlight. "As a matter of
fact, the sun is very parching sometimes in the summer and
as the little child was weak, she suffered too much from the
hot weather."

The days did not drag for the shepherd children. In fact,
time was at such a premium that their method of praying the
rosary—suggested by Jacinta—was just to say the first
words, "Our Father," then "Hail Mary" ten times and so on
through the five decades. This very efficient method of
getting finished quickly found gentle correction from the
Lady of the apparitions. Jacinta liked to gather flowers and
make a little garland for herself and Lucia. One of their
amusements when the pasture for the day was on a hill, was
to call out words and wait for an echo. Jacinta liked to call

out *Maria* as it had the best echo. She also at times called out the whole *Hail Mary*, pausing after each word to wait for the returning sound. Lucia says that Jacinta's singing voice was good.

The children had two decks of cards, one belonging to Lucia, the other to her cousins. Of all the games they played, Francisco's favorite was a card game called *bisca*. Jacinta liked to run after butterflies, and she would specify capturing a butterfly as the penalty when she won at another game called "forfeits" and had the right to determine what the loser should do.

Lucia apologizes in the Memoirs for supplying words of some of the "unholy ones" among the songs they sang. She supplied them at the wish of her spiritual director, Fr. Oliveira Galamba. Her retention of the words suggests that in her years in the convent these lovely and innocent "unholy" songs and their pastoral setting often passed wistfully through her mind. Lucia's completely human side and the naturalness of the three children comes out in her definition of nostalgia. "Nostalgia can't be described. It is a sad thorn pricking the heart for endless years. It is the remembrance of the past echoing endlessly."

Lucia describes one memory that must have floated back with a tug of the heart as she wrote it in adult years:

"Jacinta liked very much to catch the little white lambs, put them in her lap, and hug and kiss them. In the evening she would carry the smallest of them home to keep it from becoming fatigued. Coming home one day, she walked in the middle of her flock.

'Jacinta,' I asked, 'why are you walking in the midst of the sheep?'

'I'm doing what Our Lord does in the picture I was given, where He is in the middle of many with one in His arms.' "

Jacinta also gave names to the sheep, names like Dove, Star, Beauty, and Show. She had a tender heart for any creature that suffered. Before the Fatima visions she could cry over the troubles of others, over the sufferings of Jesus. One expert on her story, Fr. John DeMarchi of the Consolata Fathers, lived at Fatima for some years. He knew her parents well and interviewed them and many others as well as Sister Lucia in preparing to write his books on Fatima. He says of Jacinta: "Love worked in Jacinta like a motor, a sixteen cylinder apparatus in a very small body." She was ready for a call to the Peace Plan from Heaven, which meant love on deeper levels.

Chapter Two

The Angel of Peace

"Don't be afraid. I am the Angel of Peace." Before Heaven's Queen came to visit the three children and explain the Peace Plan in more detail, there were three preparatory visits by an angel. Their souls and the importance of the message to be committed to them for all people, evidently required this strengthening and enlightenment.

Lucia first told about the angel's visits in her second Memoir, November, 1937. The news of these visits by an angel astonished even those most fully acquainted with the Fatima events. There were three visits, all in 1916: the first probably in the spring, the second on a hot day in summer, and the third in the fall of the year. The first and third visits were on a rocky hillside of an olive grove. The rocky summit was known as the Cabezo. From it you can see much of the countryside, and can look down to the village of Aljustrel where the children lived. The second visit was at the well in Lucia's back yard.

On the day in spring when the angel first came, the three children had gone to a cave at the Cabezo for shelter from a drizzle of rain. They had finished their rosary, Lucia says possibly in the quick style, and were playing a game with little stones. A strong wind suddenly shook the trees, making them look up. They saw the figure of a young man approaching. Lucia describes him. "He was an adolescent of about 14 or 15 years of age and of great beauty. He was whiter than snow that the sun had rendered transparent as if it were made of crystal. When he approached us, he said: 'Don't be afraid. I am the Angel of Peace. Pray with me.'"

The angel then knelt and bowed his head to the ground and made them repeat three times: "My God, I believe, I adore, I hope and I love You. I beg pardon of You for those who do not believe, do not adore, do not hope and do not love You." Then the angel arose and said: "Pray thus. The hearts of Jesus and Mary are attentive to the voice of your supplications." The words of the angel made a deep impression on the children. They remained bowed down and repeated the prayer many times. Lucia asked her two cousins to keep the angel's visit a secret, which they did.

On his second visit, the angel came on a hot summer day when the children were enjoying the siesta-time shade of the overhanging fig, almond and olive trees at the well in Lucia's back yard. They were again playing. This time they did not see the angel approaching. He was suddenly beside them. He spoke.

"What are you doing? Pray, pray a great deal! The most holy hearts of Jesus and of Mary have merciful designs for you. Offer prayers and sacrifices constantly to the Most High." Lucia asked, "How are we to make sacrifices?" The angel replied: "In everything you can, offer a sacrifice as an act of reparation for sins by which He is offended, and of supplication for the conversion of sinners. Thus draw peace upon your country. I am its Guardian Angel, the Angel of Portugal. Above all, accept and endure with submission the suffering which the Lord will send you."

On his third visit the angel found the children carrying out his instructions. They had been prostrating, kneeling with their foreheads bent low to touch the ground, and repeating over and over again the angel's prayer, "O my God, I believe, I adore, I hope and I love You." They were again at the Cabezo. This time an unknown light glittered over their heads, announcing the angel's presence. Then they saw the angel, holding a chalice in his left hand. Suspended over it was a host from which drops of blood were dripping into the chalice. Leaving the chalice suspended in the air, the angel knelt beside the children, and made them repeat three times:

> Most Holy Trinity, Father, Son and Holy Spirit, I offer You the most precious Body and Blood, Soul and Divinity of Jesus Christ present in all the tabernacles of the earth, in reparation for the outrages and indifferences with which He Himself is offended. And through the infinite merits of His most Sacred Heart and of the Immaculate Heart of Mary, I beg of You the conversion of poor sinners.

Then the angel gave the Host to Lucia and divided the Blood of the chalice between Francisco and Jacinta, while he said: "Take and drink the Body and Blood of Jesus Christ, horribly insulted by ungrateful men. Make reparation for their crimes and console your God." After this the angel repeated with them, while prostrating to the ground, the new prayer, beginning, "Most Holy Trinity . . ." The children remained in the same position and continued to repeat the prayer for some time after the angel disappeared.

As in the later visions of Mary, Lucia and Jacinta saw and heard. Francisco saw but did not hear. He learned the words from the two girls. The visions of the angel had a somewhat different effect on the children than the visions of Mary. After both, they felt great peace of soul and the presence of God. But after the angel's visits they felt a certain physical weakness, and did not feel like talking about it. This feeling was strong for some days. Lucia explains the differing effects of the visits of the angel and of Mary.

"I don't know why the apparitions of Our Lady produced such different effects. There was the same intimate gladness, the same peace and happiness. But instead of that physical debility, we had a certain expansive agility; instead of that annihilation in the presence of God, an exultation of gladness; instead of that difficulty in speaking, a certain communicative enthusiasm."

So great was the feeling of the supernatural after the second appearance of the angel, that neither Lucia nor Jacinta could tell Francisco until the next day what the angel had said at the well. On the first and third visits Francisco, of course, heard the words of the prayer and joined in them as the two girls prayed aloud. When the children did talk about the angel, the strange, strong feeling would return. "I don't know what it is that I feel," said Jacinta, "but I can't talk or play or sing, or anything." Francisco said in reply, "It doesn't matter. The angel is better than anything. Let's think of him."

The visits of the angel were definite mystical experiences. We are all much closer to God than we ordinarily imagine. "In him we live and move and have our being" (Ac 17:18). Angels are also always near us. It is not surprising that at times they make their presence known in ways that the senses of man can pick up. Lucia, in fact, had a special reason when the angel first came to her and her two cousins for requesting silence. She had already had an angel-experience that caused her a little difficulty with her family. When she first started shepherding her parents' flock (probably in 1915) she and three companions, Teresa and Maria Rosa Matias and Maria Justino went to the Cabezo. About noon when they had begun saying a rosary, a visible figure hung in the air before them over the grove of trees. "It was a figure like a statue made of snow that the rays from the sun had turned somewhat transparent." The four girls continued to pray with eyes fixed on the figure. It disappeared as they finished the rosary. The other three girls told their families, though Lucia said nothing. The news got around to Lucia's mother, Maria Rosa. She leveled a stern finger and called it "silly girls' nonsense." Her sisters made fun of her too because of this reported incident. "Are you seeing somebody wrapped up in a sheet?" they had asked when Lucia looked abstracted after her first Holy Communion.

There is an interesting speculation to make here. Did God perhaps turn from other possible "Fatima children" who did not match up to the first mystical overture of an angel? Did God then seek out Lucia's younger cousins? Perhaps Francisco and Jacinta were substitutes who proved worthy and made the rightly balanced response. There is between God and his frail creature, man, a fine line of harmonious communication. It involves the mystery of man's freedom of choice. The Spirit breathes where He will. His messengers, the angels, wait for consent as Gabriel waited at Nazareth.

Mystical experiences are not unusual in the lives of people called to do something special for God. Padre Pio, the Italian Capuchin priest, bore the visible marks of Christ's wounds in his hands and feet and side for 50 years. Many American soldiers saw him during World War II. Brother Andre who died in Montreal in 1937, helped thousands of people in extraordinary ways with a certainty that was a gift of God, a mystical knowledge beyond ordinary human prudence.

A touch of the mystical enters the lives of many people. The external phenomena are not present, but there is a deepening of the sense of God's presence, a new awareness

of a world beyond the visible, a stronger sense of call. Only
God knows how great may be the multitude of people very
close to Him. Over-involvement in the material and the
sensual tends to hinder the mystical. Prayer, deliberate penance, or suffering unsought but accepted in a humble spirit
ordinarily set up the condition of soul which invites the
mystical.

Every person, created a little less than the angels, reaches
out for something beyond this world. Man, made in the
image of his Maker, reaches out for God. The momentary
pull, the uplift, the sense of being possessed by an angelic
force fades. But the yearning remains, strengthened and
naked, left to cope with the still insistent demands of the
mundane.

Jacinta felt some of all this in a child's way. But after the
visits of the angel and of Mary, she remained a child. The
angel's visits made a change, deepening her interest in the
sufferings of Jesus. She asked Lucia more often to describe
them to her. She had a growing awareness that His sufferings were the payment for sins. There was a growing awareness and understanding too that sins caused wars, and that
prayer and sacrifice helped to end them or prevent them.

Still Mary found the children praying the rapid rosary,
as suggested by Jacinta, and surely not seconded by the
angel. Jacinta had to assimilate the mystical with the tools of
a child's intelligence, logic, experience and emotions. When
the children were in jail over the 13th of August, her great
fear and pain were not of being boiled in oil as was
threatened, but from thinking her parents had deserted
them. She wept over this. "We'll die without even seeing our
parents. They haven't even come to see us. That's how much
they care."

In the half year from the third visit of the angel till
Mary's first visit, Jacinta had time to assimilate the message,

think and grow spiritually. She remained the same spontaneous child of effervescent joy or immediate sorrow. She entered into the situation at hand with laughter or weeping. But after the angel's visits there was a new bond between the three children. Especially in Jacinta there was a stronger tendency to shy away from playing with and talking with the other children who might be around. She needed more the support of Lucia and wanted more the company of Francisco. Her aloneness reached out to feel the courage her companions in the mystical event were able to give her.

Chapter Three

The Lady of Light

The time had come in God's plans for the stronger and deeper and still more beautiful experiences of the three children. These were the six appearances of the one who with a mother's love had stood at the foot of the cross of Jesus. Now, with a mother's love for all, she wanted through the children, to call all to prayer and repentance, and the peace it would bring. Each time she came there was a flash of light that preceded and bespoke her near presence. At times, others besides the children saw this light. When she left, she went with a growing brightness that dimmed the sun and allowed the thousands on October 13th to look at it without harm to their eyes.

Mary at Fatima has been called the Lady of Light. Besides the light that was visible to others at times, she also opened her hands several times during the series of visions, and rays of light flowed from them to penetrate the children, bringing light and understanding about important truths, and a sense of happiness and peace.

On Sunday, May 13, 1917 the children went to early Mass. Then they took the sheep to pasture and said their usual speedy rosary. They were playing at building castles out of rocks. The nonchalant Francisco had been generously allotted the more desirable position. Jacinta and Lucia gathered the stones. Francisco did the building. They saw a sudden shaft of light which frightened them. They thought it might portend a storm, and started to gather the sheep and prepare to go home. Another shaft of light cut the cloudless air, and then, standing over a holm oak was a most beautiful Lady, "dressed all in white, more brilliant than the sun . . ."

"Fear not, I will not harm you," the Lady said. Lucia asked where she was from. "I am from heaven." "What do you want?" Lucia asked. Jacinta never spoke to the Lady all through the visions. She just listened. "I came to ask you to come here for six consecutive months, on the 13th day, at this same hour. I will tell you later who I am and what I want. And I shall return here again a seventh time."

"And I, am I too going to go to heaven?" Lucia asked. "Yes, you shall." "And Jacinta?" "Yes." "And Francisco?" "He too shall go, but he must say many rosaries." Francisco at this moment saw and was surrounded by the light that denoted the Lady's presence, but could not see her. He suggested throwing a stone to see if what Lucia talked to was real. Lucia passed on to him the Lady's suggestion that he say the rosary: "Let him say the rosary, and in that way, he too will see me." Francisco took out his rosary and by the time he had finished one decade, he saw the Lady.

Jacinta in her child's way thought the Lady might be hungry after coming so far. "Lucia, ask the Lady if she is hungry. We still have some bread and cheese." Francisco began to worry about the sheep eating vegetables from a neighbor's garden. Lucia told him that the Lady said they would not, and Francisco relaxed.

Lucia then asked about two girls who had recently died, whether or not they were in heaven. The Lady said one was, the other was in purgatory. The Lady then asked the question: "Do you want to offer yourselves to God to endure all the sufferings He may choose to send you, as an act of reparation for the sins by which He is offended and as a supplication for the conversion of sinners?" Lucia said: "Yes, we do." "Then you are going to suffer a great deal, but the grace of God will be your comfort."

At this time the Lady opened her hands and light came as though glancing from them into the children. "This light," Lucia would report from the vantage point of adult years, "penetrated us to the heart and its very recesses, and allowed us to see ourselves in God, Who was that light, more clearly than we see ourselves in a mirror. Then we were moved by an inner impulse, also communicated to us, to fall on our knees, while we repeated to ourselves: 'Most Holy Trinity, I adore you. My God, my God, I love you in the Most Blessed Sacrament.'"

The Lady's final words on May 13th were: "Say the rosary every day to earn peace for the world and the end of the war." (It must be kept in mind that World War One was raging at the time of the visions.) The Lady elevated herself and disappeared gradually as she went toward the east, "still surrounded by a most brilliant light that seemed to open a path for her through the myriad galaxies of stars."

The Lady did not ask them to keep this visit a secret, but they agreed solemnly to tell no one. Lucia knew full well that her mother, Maria Rosa, would not take kindly to such a story. Jacinta kept the promise of secrecy exactly till she caught sight of her parents returning from Batalha that evening. She ran to her mother and exploded into a rapid description of the vision of the Lady in the Cova da Iria. She demonstrated by holding her hands in imitation of how the Lady folded her hands and held a rosary. "When she went back to heaven," Jacinta concluded, "the doors seemed to shut so quickly that I thought that her feet would get caught. . ."

There was much discussion in the Marto family that night. It was a big family. Senhora Olympia had mothered 11 children, 2 from a first marriage and 9 in her marriage to Senhor Marto. Jacinta as the youngest had a happy time of babyhood being bounced from lap to lap and cuddled and made over. Now the baby of the family had something beside childhood charms to offer, an amazing story. The boys laughed at their little sister. The girls were fascinated. Olympia made light of the matter. Ti Marto, a very steady, moderate man summed up: "From the beginning of time Our Lady has appeared many times and in many ways. This is what has been helping us. If the world is in bad shape today, it would be worse, had there not been cases of this sort. The power of God is great."

Gradually the news spread from Olympia. She had dutifully scolded Jacinta, but with a tongue-in-cheek attitude, she told the neighbors. The circle reached Lucia through her oldest sister, Maria dos Angelos. Maria was twenty at the time. She relates:

"The first rumors of something extraordinary alleged to have happened at the Cova to my sister Lucia and her two younger cousins Franciso and Jacinta, came to us from our neighbors. We were very upset when we heard the gist of it—visions of Our Lady or something of that kind—for they were not unnaturally inclined to make fun of the children, since as you well know, we are very matter-of-fact and common-sense people around these parts, and nothing would make us a greater laughing stock than fanciful tales like this on the part of our children. I did not say anything to Lucia at first but watched her. She seemed more serious and preoccupied than was normal for a ten-year-old, but otherwise she was natural and cheerful enough. After several days I felt sure she had something extraordinary on her mind . . . I sat down beside her and began to lead up to the subject in a roundabout way, telling her about the absurd talk and rumors that were going about the village. She was very upset and wondered how the matter had got out, for she said the three of them had agreed to keep it secret. I told her it seemed that Jacinta had not been able to contain herself . . ."

Lucia's father Antonio Santos was nicknamed "the pumpkin" around Aljustrel. He was somewhat noted for his ease at raising the bottle in the village tavern. He steered clear of the rumpus by saying that it was all a bunch of women talking. Her mother Maria Rosa, a devout and strict person, and not in good health did some talking, most of it directed at Lucia for lying. Things went hard for Lucia all during the series of visions. They began in a situation already hard on her family. Her father had lost some of their land. Two older sisters had left to get married, leaving their accustomed work for the family behind. Her mother was diagnosed as having a heart lesion, bad kidneys and a dislocation in her spine. Lucia, in fact, had just lately inherited the job of shepherdess, due to these family changes. Little wonder that Lucia's mother found unbearable the troubles caused by visions she believed were inventions of the children. The parish priest, Fr. Manuel Ferreira, was irritated by the whole affair. "So far I have never had to listen to anything of this sort. Everybody knows things before me."

As time went on, the children were caught between the good-hearted and the mean, the devout and the skeptical. Some people ridiculed them. Some even threw stones. As the months went on, crowds came to trample down the pasture land. Their horses helped themselves to the sheep's grass. Eventually, the sheep had to be sold. The children were besieged by endless questioners. They were called the Pope's puppets. Following the lead of Maria Rosa, some of the village women did not hesitate to box Lucia's ears. Ti Marto's firm fatherhood protected her cousins. Jacinta, eager for sacrifice, confided to Lucia: "I wish my parents were like yours. Then I could get beaten too, and I would have another sacrifice to offer Our Lord."

On the first Monday, May 14, 1917, all these things were just beginning. As is the usual pattern of life, the biggest sacrifices would come from outside the immediate control of the will—from other people, from circumstances, from sickness. The three children, generous and in the fresh strength of the Lady of Light, did not wait for sacrifices to come. That first day, at Francisco's suggestion, they made the sacrifice of giving the sheep their lunch. The sheep feasted on the sandwiches, and the children ate some acorns, edible but bitter to the taste. In the days and months to come they often gave away their lunch to some poor children. They ate fruit from the trees, pine seeds, bind-weed roots and olives.

Often they waited when thirsty and offered this up for sinners and for peace. One sunny afternoon their thirst prompted them to ask at a nearby house for water. The good lady there gave them a jug of water and a piece of bread. Lucia gave the jug to Francisco. He said, "I don't want to drink . . . I want to suffer for sinners. You drink, Jacinta." And Jacinta also turned from the tempting drink. "I want to offer a sacrifice for sinners too." Lucia poured the water into a rock hollow for the sheep and returned the jug. The heat became more intense. Cicadas and crickets joined forces with the frogs in the nearby lagoon, making an intolerable clamor. "Tell the crickets and the frogs to be silent. I have a terrible headache," said Jacinta. Francisco asked: "Don't you want to offer this up for sinners?" And Jacinta, pressing her head between her hands answered, "Yes, I do. Let them sing."

Maria Rosa, as pressure on her family grew, berated Lucia for lying more insistently, and even took the broom to her. "How can I say I was lying?" Lucia asked in tears when she met her little cousins. Francisco reproached Jacinta. "Do you see? You are guilty of this. Why did you tell them?" Jacinta began to cry, knelt down and lifted up her hands to beg pardon. "I did wrong, but I won't say any more to anybody." Lucia, recounting this in the first Memoir, remarks on this unusual act of humility. "In my opinion, Jacinta was the one whom the Blessed Virgin granted a greater abundance of graces and a better knowledge of God and virtue."

Maria Rosa took Lucia to the parish priest one morning with instructions to get down on her knees and tell the priest she had been lying. On the way she stopped to see Olympia, her sister-in-law. (Lucia's father and Jacinta's mother were brother and sister.) Lucia had a chance then to tell Jacinta about what was going on. Jacinta called Francisco and the two prayed by the well in Lucia's back yard, until Lucia and her mother returned. Jacinta then ran to hug her cousin and ask how things went. Hearing that Lucia stood firm, Jacinta said: "You see, we ought never to be afraid of anything. That Lady will always protect us. She is such a good friend of ours."

There was nothing stereotyped about the way the children accepted the Lady of the visions. They sometimes referred to her as *Our Lady* and sometimes as *That Lady*. As Jacinta said in such a simple, matter-of-fact way, and very unchurchy—That Lady is such a good friend of ours.

As the various difficulties turned up, Jacinta, wanting to waste no chance to help poor sinners, used to ask: "Did you already say to Jesus that this is for His love?" If Lucia's answer was "No," she would say, "Then I will say it to Him." She would join her hands, raise her eyes to heaven, and say,

"Jesus, this is for your love and the conversion of sinners."

June 13th was a big day at the Fatima parish. It was the feastday of St. Anthony, the parish patron. The weather was clear and quite hot. After Mass the Martos went off to market, the Santos went to the parish festivities. A crowd of about 50 persons, some devout, some curious—including 14 girlfriends invited by Lucia—followed her and her two cousins to the Cova. Maria Correira of Moita came, bringing her 17-year-old crippled son, John. Later she would be known as Maria de Capelinha (Mary of the Chapel), and would take care of the little Fatima chapel. The group prayed the rosary. About noon Maria de Capelinha heard Lucia cry out: "Jacinta, there comes Our Lady. There is the light." Maria de Capelinha and some others also "heard something like a small, small voice, but could not understand what it was trying to say," as she later testified. Maria de Capelinha was quite helpful through many years to pilgrims and to authors who were gathering data about the events at Fatima.

On that June 13th the Lady taught the children the prayer many millions of people have used since between the decades of the rosary. "O my Jesus, forgive us our sins, save us from the fires of hell. And lead all souls to heaven, especially those who have most need of your mercy." The Lady told Lucia that she wanted her to learn to read and write. She promised that a certain sick man would be cured within a year if he converted. Lucia asked: "Will you take us to heaven?"

"Yes, I will take Jacinta and Francisco soon. You, however, will remain here for a longer time. Jesus wants to use you to make me known and loved. He wants to establish the Devotion to my Immaculate Heart in the world. I promise salvation to those who embrace it and their souls will be loved by God as flowers placed by myself to adorn His throne." When Lucia asked tearfully if she were to be all alone, the Lady said: "Does this cause you to suffer a great deal? I will never leave you. My Immaculate Heart will be your refuge and the way that will lead you to God."

Then the Lady, as she had done on her first visit, opened her hands. Lucia describes this and interprets it in the third Memoir:

"She opened her hands and pierced our hearts with the light that streamed from her palms. It seems then that the first purpose of this light was to give us a special knowledge of and a special love for the Immaculate Heart of Mary just as on two other occasions it gave us a better knowledge of God and the mystery of the Holy Trinity. From that day on we felt in our hearts a deeper love for the Immaculate Heart of Mary."

In the fourth Memoir Lucia tells of a question Francisco asked after the June 13th apparition. "Why was Our Lady, with a Heart in her hand, scattering on the world such a great light which was God? You were with Our Lady in the light which was coming down to the ground, and Jacinta and I were in the light which was going up to the sky." Lucia explained that this was so because he and Jacinta would soon be going to heaven, while she would stay with the Immaculate Heart of Mary on earth.

Maria de Capelinha describes the ending of Our Lady's June visit:

"Lucia got up very quickly and with her arm stretched out, cried, 'Look, there she goes. There she goes.' We saw nothing except a little cloud a few inches from the tree which rose very slowly and went backwards, towards the east, until we could see it no more. . . . We then turned toward the miraculous tree, and what was our admiration and surprise to see that the shoots at the top, which had been standing upright before, were now all bent toward the east, as if someone had stood upon them. Then we began to pull off twigs and leaves from the top of the tree, but Lucia told us to take them from the bottom where Our Lady had not touched them."

The group of fifty prayed the litany of the Blessed Virgin before leaving the Cova, and then broke up to go to their various homes or other destinations. Maria de Capelinha and the three children and some others went to the parish church and arrived just in time for the St. Anthony procession. As the children went home later after the festivities at the parish, they began to pay more of the price of their choice by heaven for a special work. "What, still on earth?" "Haven't you gone to heaven yet?" "Jacinta, that cat still have your tongue?" "Did the Lady speak with you?" "Are you a saint yet, Jacinta?"

Chapter Four

The Secret

The time between the June and July visions was the most critical for the series of Mary's Fatima visits because one of the visionaries almost lost courage. Lucia, in fact, had already determined not to go back to the Cova for the July meeting with the Lady. We can judge the extent of her misery in reaching this decision by weighing it against the special graces of God already given and her earlier enthusiasm. She left the June meeting refreshed, strengthened, glowing. She approached the time of the promised July visit by telling her cousins that she wasn't going.

Jacinta unconsciously had something to do with causing the trouble. She also had much to do with finally winning Lucia back to do the Lady's bidding. After the June visit Jacinta longed to tell her mother the whole story, especially that the Lady promised to take her and Francisco to heaven soon. But she confined herself to describing the Lady's beauty. The family brought out pictures, and referred to various statues and living women. "Was she more beautiful than . . . ?" The answer always was "Much more beautiful."

Jacinta was talking about the Lady's beauty. In the back of her mind was the delightful thought of seeing her always in heaven, and the prediction that soon the Lady would take her and Francisco there. Thinking of this prediction, Jacinta used one word that has had a strong effect on the rest of the Fatima story for her and the other children, for their families and for millions since. "She told us a secret that we cannot tell," said Jacinta. That did it. Interest everywhere intensified, beginning in the Marto family. Everybody but Ti Marto tried to find out what the secret was. He said, "A secret is a secret and it should be kept." Actually the Blessed Virgin had not asked the children to keep anything secret. It was in the next month that she would tell them not to relate, for the time being, certain parts of her message. After that, Jacinta, the little girl who couldn't keep from blurting out in the beginning, was ready to die rather than tell the items the Blessed Virgin had required silence about. In August, literally threatened to be boiled alive in oil by the Administrator of Ourem if they did not tell him "the secret," all three children kept it.

Had Mary spoken to adults, possibly they would prudently never have used the term, *secret*, which stirred so much trouble. They may have just related what happened and kept quiet about everything that was not to be related. In fact, not only adults, but Lucia and Francisco would have done this. It is, on looking back, rather ridiculous that a tug of war should have resulted between such little ones and the County Administrator and others who professed not to believe in the visions at all. If they did not believe, why try to learn a secret which was just part of a few children's imaginative game? It was also rather unfeeling that those who did believe, should press anyone, especially children, to tell what the Blessed Virgin had said to keep quiet. Ti Marto was the most sensible. "A secret is a secret and it should be kept."

If Jacinta had been in advertising or public relations, she could have picked no better word to catch interest and promote discussion and controversy. From hamlet to hamlet in the surrounding country, the news spread. The result was that on July 13th, a crowd numbering in the thousands was out at the Cova da Iria, awaiting whatever would happen. Alarmed at the sight of all the people going by on donkey and mule, and fearing for their children's safety, the two mothers, Olympia and Maria Rosa, decided to go themselves but remain in the background, hidden and unidentified. They carried blessed candles against any possible manifestation of the devil.

That is what was causing the trouble for Lucia—the devil. Her mother had taken her and her cousins to Fr. Ferreira to be questioned. He had asked that the children be brought as the whole thing was blowing up to such unusual proportions. Maria Rosa hoped that the good pastor would get to the truth of the matter and settle once for all the big rumpus so her family could live again in peace. Jacinta took out a rosary and said nothing at her interview. Francisco said very little. Lucia defended the truth of the Lady's appearances. The children were kindly received at the rectory by the pastor and his sister. The good man simply did not know what to make of his young parishioners. Perhaps there was another intelligence behind them. He did not doubt their sincerity. But the news that reached him of their clever handling of all questioners made him wonder if perhaps the devil might not, for the joy of skeptics and others who ridiculed the Church, be setting up a scene to harm souls. They warned Lucia about the deceits of the devil. Maria Rosa did not let her daughter forget about the warning. So Lucia got to the point of confusion. For awhile she thought the best thing to do would be to say that it was all a lie. She began to wonder if it could be the devil.

Jacinta said: "No, no, it could not be the devil. People say the devil is very ugly and lives under the earth in hell, but that Lady was so beautiful . . ." Jacinta and Franciso both argued with Lucia in this manner. The two little ones decided they would go without Lucia. Jacinta even agreed to talk to the Lady. Lucia gave her instructions: "If she asks about me, tell her I'm afraid it is the devil who sends her to us." But at the last moment, Lucia's doubts and fears suddenly vanished; she ran to her cousins' house to find Jacinta and Francisco kneeling at the bed, praying and crying. Their courage without her was vanishing. They could not make up their minds to start for the Cova. Now they all three ran joyfully. The devil had almost won. Perhaps he knew that some of his secrets were going to be exposed on that day.

Lucia tells about the famous Fatima secret in the third Memoir. The chief purpose of this Memoir was to elucidate some details of Jacinta's life. Lucia writes: "Well, the secret is composed of three different parts, two of which I will go on to reveal. The first is the vision of hell . . . The second part refers to the devotion to the Immaculate Heart of Mary . . ."

The secret was revealed to the children in the July apparition. The fact that Lucia links the secret closely to Jacinta shows that the July visit of Mary, with its strong emphasis on hell and devotion to the Immaculate Heart, provides a clue to understanding Jacinta. From July onward, Jacinta's struggle toward spiritual maturity centered on these truths. In her letter to the Bishop of Leiria that accompanied the third Memoir, Lucia in fact suggested that the book *Jacinta*, soon to be published, should have one chapter entitled "Hell" and another on the "Immaculate Heart of Mary."

The external events of the July vision are described by Ti Marto, as written down by Fr. John DeMarchi. "I left home determined to see what would happen. I could not believe the children were telling lies. How many times I had said to my sister-in-law, 'Maria Rosa, if people say all this is just the invention of the parents, you and I know it is not true. We have never encouraged them one bit, and even Fr. Ferreira says it could be the work of the devil.' " In this remark about gossip accusing the parents, Jacinta's father opens a new window on the pressures placed on the children's families. He continues:

"But what a crowd of people were there that day. I could not see the children because there were so many people in the Cova by the tree. I kept getting closer to them, and then I could see two men, one of them from Ramila and the other from Fatima, trying to make a barrier around the children so they would not be crushed. These men saw me and they grabbed my arm, and they called to the crowd, 'Here is the father, let him through.' And so down by the oak tree I got close to my Jacinta. Lucia I could see a little way off. She was saying the rosary, and the people were responding aloud. When the beads were finished, she jumped up suddenly. 'Close your umbrellas,' she called to the people who were using them to shade the strong sunlight, 'Our Lady is coming.' She was looking to the east, and I was too, but I could not see anything at first. But then I saw what looked like a little greyish cloud resting on the oak tree. The heat of the sun was suddenly less severe. A fine fresh breeze was blowing, and it did not seem like the height of summer. The people were silent, terribly silent, and then I began to hear a sound, a little buzzing sound it was, like a mosquito in a bottle. I could not hear any words, but just this buzzing. I have often thought that talking on the phone must sound like that, though I have never talked on one. What is this buzzing? I asked myself. Is it near or far away?"

The buzzing sound or the sound of a low muffled voice and the little cloud coming, hovering and going away, were noticed by many people present at Mary's later visits. Fr. DeMarchi gives an apt comment: "Exactly why God chooses to draw His pictures dimly for some, and with the powerful light of creation for others, we do not pretend to know."

At Mary's July visit, Jacinta told Lucia: "Speak, Our Lady is talking to you." Lucia asked the Lady, "What do you want of me?"

"I want you to come back here on the thirteenth of next month. Continue to say the rosary every day in honor of Our Lady of the Rosary, to obtain the peace of the world and the end of the war, because only she can obtain it." Lucia then asked if the Lady would do something to make certain to the people that she really came and spoke to her and Francisco and Jacinta. She also asked if the Lady would tell her name. The reply was: "You must come here every month, and in October I will tell you who I am and what I want. I will then perform a miracle so that all may believe."

Among the many special questions about possible cures that Lucia then relayed to the Blessed Virgin for various people was one about the son of Maria de Capelinha. Mary replied that he would not be cured, nor his poverty changed. He must make certain to say the rosary daily with his family. (John Carreira remained crippled, and later became sacristan of the chapel in the Cova.)

"Sacrifice yourselves for sinners; and say often, especially when you make some sacrifice: 'My Jesus, it is for love of You, for the conversion of sinners, and in reparation for sins committed against the Immaculate Heart of Mary.'" After this admonition, Mary opened her hands as she had done twice before. The light reflecting from them seemed to penetrate the earth. This was now the moment of giving the secret. Lucia describes what the children saw.

"Our Lady showed us a large sea of fire which seemed to be beneath the earth. Plunged in this fire were the demons and the souls, who were like embers, transparent and black or bronze-colored, with human forms which floated about in the conflagration, borne by the flames which issued from it with clouds of smoke, falling on all sides as sparks fall in great conflagrations, without weight or equilibrium, among shrieks and groans of sorrow and despair, which horrified us and caused us to quake with fear. The devils were distinguished by horrible and loathsome forms of animals, frightful and unknown, but transparent and black. This vision vanished in a moment. Providentially, our good heavenly Mother had promised us in the first apparition to take us to heaven. Otherwise, I think we would have died of fright and horror."

"Shortly afterwards we raised our eyes to Our Lady who said with goodness and sadness, 'You have seen hell, where the souls of poor sinners go. To save them, God wishes to establish in the world the devotion to the Immaculate Heart. If they do what I will tell you, many souls will be saved, and there will be peace. The war is going to end. But if they don't stop offending God, another and worse one will begin in the reign of Pius XI. When you shall see a night illuminated by an unknown light, know that this is the great sign that God will give you, that He is going to punish the world by means of war, hunger and persecutions of the Church, and of the Holy Father. To prevent this, I shall come to ask for the consecration of Russia to my Immaculate Heart; and for the Communion of Reparation on the First Saturdays. If they listen to my requests, Russia will be converted, and there will be peace. If not she will scatter her errors throughout the world, provoking wars and persecutions of the Church. The good will be martyred, the Holy Father will have much to suffer, and various nations will be annihilated. In the end, my Immaculate Heart will triumph. The Holy Father will consecrate Russia to me, and she will be converted, and a certain period of peace will be granted to the world.' " (See Appendix B).

The July vision made the most impression on Jacinta.

We might say that the Blessed Virgin led this child of grace through hell in order to lead many others to heaven; took her to the place where there is no peace, in order to help the human race find peace on earth. But this revelation was only after two assurances of the children's going to heaven, made in May and June. So, Jacinta did not have to worry about herself, that she might be lost and have to join the souls and devils so frighteningly portrayed in her great mystical experience. First, an angel had strengthened the souls of the children; then the gentle voice of Mary had spoken words of reassurance and promise, and further strengthened them by the graces of divine illumination symbolized by the rays of light.

Lucia answers the question of many concerning what brought Jacinta to such a high degree of understanding about prayer and penance, and to such a willingness to make sacrifices. "In my opinion, it was, first of all through a special grace God granted her through the Immaculate Heart of Mary; and secondly, through the vision of hell, and the unfortunate souls falling into it."

Towards the end of her trek to spiritual maturity, shortly before she went to the hospital, Jacinta encouraged Lucia not to be afraid to proclaim at the proper time the specialized information about God's will. The immediately to-be-proclaimed part of the Peace Plan was to amend one's life, to stop sinning, to pray and offer sacrifices for those who do not amend. The great secret given to the children, is that peace and the Immaculate Heart of Mary are very much intertwined in God's plans for mankind. Jacinta then, in her last months speaks as the little veteran, the pioneer who had understood and done exactly what God wants. She told Lucia not to fear proclaiming the secret.

"It won't be long before I go to heaven. You are to stay here to make known Our Lord's desire to establish in the world the devotion to the Immaculate Heart of Mary. When the time comes to speak, you mustn't hold back, but tell everybody that God granted graces to us through the Immaculate Heart of Mary, that we must ask her for them, that the Heart of Jesus wishes to be honored together with the Immaculate Heart, *because God has entrusted peace to her*. Oh, if I could only put into everybody's heart the burning fire I have inside me which makes me love the Hearts of Jesus and Mary so much."

Why would God want to entrust peace to the Immaculate Heart of Mary? Isn't this just a mumbo-jumbo way of speaking? Is it so esoteric that only a few devout Catholics or trained theologians can understand it? Or is it something that a great many can understand? The children understood that devotion to Mary's Immaculate Heart and its connection with peace was really a revelation. In fact, this is the major secret of Fatima, now no longer hidden, but open for examination. Jesus said: "If you love me, keep my commandments." He gave love as the criterion and substance of the moral order. The message at Fatima is: If you love, keep your heart like that of Mary.

In the July vision of hell, the children by special illumination saw self-love undisguised and naked, consuming itself as a flame from within. They heard envy, jealousy, pride, greed, lust and the assorted choir of all the vices shouting and shrieking and screaming in the disharmony and harshness of their own intimate natures. They saw the final state of those called to love who make a final, unchangeable choice not to love. They saw the disorder of sin undisguised by its usual trappings, as it is in its essence.

The graphic illustration the three children saw, portrayed a core reality. They went through a deep mystical experience. We don't have to accept that what Lucia describes and what she and Francisco and Jacinta saw was the visible reality of hell. They were made to understand by illustration the meaning of hell, its lack of peace and love, its total disorder from what man values and what makes him happy. Actually, Lucia says that what she has written does not approach even the reality of what they saw.

Often Jacinta sat on the ground or on a stone meditating. "Hell! Hell! How sorry I am for the souls that are going to hell. And people burn there alive, like wood in fire!" Then she would kneel and raise her hands and say the prayer taught by the Lady to use between decades of the rosary. "O my Jesus, pardon us, save us from the fires of hell, and lead all souls to heaven, especially those most in need of Your mercy."

Many times Jacinta asked what kind of sins people committed that made them go to hell. Lucia would recite the sins evident to a child's eyes. "Perhaps not going to Mass on Sundays, stealing, saying wicked words, cursing, swearing." "And only for one word they can go to hell?" Jacinta asked. "What would it cost them to keep quiet and go to Mass? I am sorry for sinners. Oh, if I could only let them see hell!"

Jacinta also asked, "Why doesn't Our Lady show hell to sinners? If they saw it, they would never sin again and wouldn't have to go there. You must tell that Lady to show hell to all those people." She was speaking of the people who came to the Cova at the time of the apparitions. "You will see that they will be converted."

When, in the later days of her sickness, Jacinta wanted to mortify herself and not eat, Lucia at times said: "Jacinta, come on, eat now." And Jacinta replied: "No, I am offering this sacrifice for those who eat too much." She said the same when going to weekday Mass: "I will go for sinners who don't go even on Sundays." At times she covered her face with her hands on hearing loud cursing. "O my God, don't these people realize this kind of talk might send them to hell? Forgive them, Jesus and convert them. They certainly don't know they are offending God."

Sometimes she hugged Lucia and said: "I am going to heaven, but you have to stay here. If Our Lady lets you, tell everybody what hell is like, so that they can escape it by not committing sins." Lucia tried to reassure her: "Don't be afraid, you are going to heaven." "Yes, I am going there. But I also want everyone to go there."

Jacinta thought much. Often Lucia found her in a pensive mood and asked what she might be thinking about. Often Jacinta answered: "Of that war which is coming, of the many people who are going to die and go to hell. What a shame! If they would stop offending God, neither the war would come, nor would they go to hell." Sometimes the comment is made: "War is hell." Jacinta linked war and hell together for she knew they both came from the disorder of sin, and both could be prevented by turning to the order and love that was the complete opposite of war and hell, the Immaculate Heart of Mary.

So Jacinta pondered. Like Mary at Nazareth she loved to think. Often she sat for long periods in the parish church before the "hidden Jesus" and tried to fit all the pieces together. Gradually the Holy Spirit led her on. She was conscious of hell as representing God's justice, of the Immaculate Heart as representing His mercy. At opposite poles in representing order and disorder in the creature, they are also at opposite poles in showing God's justice and mercy. Mary's Heart gives us an idea of God's pursuing love for each person. Hell gives an idea of His pursuing justice which demands a restoration beyond our comprehension.

In her last weeks Jacinta reports Our Lady as saying: "I can no longer restrain the hand of my divine Son." She also said: "Our Lady cannot at present avert the justice of her Son from the world." This is not to imply that there is some opposition between Jesus and Mary. Nor does it mean that she is more merciful than Christ. All through the Fatima story the two Hearts go together, as they do in correct theology. "The Heart of Jesus wishes to be honored together with the Immaculate Heart because God has entrusted peace to her," said Jacinta. "Oh, if I could only put into everybody's heart the burning fire I have inside me which makes me love the Hearts of Jesus and Mary so much!"

The expressions of apparent opposition are adapted to the minds of many people. They picture the feminine heart as softer than the masculine. The expressions also suggest God's plan which in working out the mysterious balance of justice and mercy allows creatures a share in His loving Providence. In fact, God calls us also to a share in swinging the balance to mercy. We are in His plans too, called to join the Immaculate Heart in winning mercy for souls. Jacinta had a strong grasp on this truth, so central to the whole meaning of Fatima. To join the Immaculate Heart of Mary, adding and making more pure and fervent our desires for mercy—this is the Peace Plan, the way to save men from war and souls from hell.

At Fatima God used hell and the Immaculate Heart in a startling drama to show two very important things about Himself. His justice is stern as the flames of hell. His mercy is as yearning as the Heart of the most perfect and tender among women. And they are one. In our minds they are in conflict, especially when it comes to the vivid showing of hell. Drama is based on the resolution of a conflict. In Jacinta, the youngest prophet, we have the resolution of the conflict as the curtain comes down on the great drama of Fatima. If we can understand her, we have taken a step forward in solving for ourselves the age-old conflict posed in the question: How can a good and merciful God punish forever? She accepted hell completely and literally as shown in the vision. She accepted God's pursuing mercy completely as shown in the Immaculate Heart.

Her response was to turn to the Heart of Jesus: "O my Jesus, forgive us our sins, save us from the fires of hell, and lead all souls to heaven, especially those who have most need of Your mercy." Her response was more sacrifice and prayer. Her response was to bow to the ground and say: "O Most Holy Trinity, I believe in You, I adore You, hope in You and love You. I wish to make amends for those who do not believe, do not adore, hope and love."

Chapter Five

Kidnapped

The 13th of August found the three children in jail. Maria dos Anjos, Lucia's oldest sister, tells what happened at the Cova da Iria. "On the 13th of August, the children by a trick were whisked off to Ourem and threatened with torture and death if they would not confess to perpetrating a hoax. Knowing nothing of this, but supposing the children were going to be taken to the Cova after visiting the parish priest, we and a very big crowd gathered at the usual spot." The crowd was estimated by the Catholic regional paper, *A Liberdade*, at from 5,000 to 15,000. Maria continues:

"It may seem strange that this time, when the children did not arrive, I and many others experienced certain signs and strong impressions of the supernatural, and this is the time when our faith was really born. There seemed to be a cloud over the little tree at noon; also noises like explosions, and a trembling like an earthquake. At least we could not now blame the children for any of these things. We were all very afraid and impressed . . . There was also a kind of colorfulness all round, and what seemed like colored petals, floating in the air, but not reaching the ground. We all left, feeling very chastened for our lack of faith, but now believing fully and deeply."

Maria da Capelinha also has left a statement about what happened at the Cova on August 13, 1917.

"The crowd this day was greater than it had been in July. Oh, there were many, many more. Some came on foot and hung their bundles on the trees. Some came on horses. Some on mules. There were bicycles too . . . All around the tree, the people were praying and singing hymns, but when the children did not appear they began to get impatient. Then someone came from Fatima and told us they had been kidnapped by the Mayor. Everyone began talking at once; there was great anger, and I don't know what would have happened if we hadn't heard the clap of thunder . . . Just after the clap of thunder came a flash of lightning, and then we began to see a little cloud, very delicate, very white, which stopped for a few moments over the tree, and then rose in the air until it disappeared. As we looked around, we began to notice some strange things we had observed before and would see again in the months to follow. Our faces were reflecting all the colors of the rainbow—pink and red and blue and I don't know what. The trees suddenly seemed to be made not of leaves but of flowers. The ground reflected these many colors and so did the clothes we wore."

Maria da Capelinha and Maria, sister of Lucia were convinced that Our Lady had come at her usual time around the noon hour. So were most of the large crowd of several thousand who had seen these signs. Before long, some of them as they talked things over became an angry, perhaps even a dangerous mob. Their anger was directed at the Administrator of Ourem and also at the parish priest who they thought was his accomplice in kidnapping the children.

At this time the children were in the county seat of Ourem, kidnapped by the County Administrator, Arturo de Oliveira Santos. As a fallen-away Catholic actively working against the Faith, he had much at stake. He enjoyed his reputation as an enemy of the Church and all similar superstitions. He did not want to be made the laughing-stock of Portugal. Feared by the people, he was a local tyrant who held all the political power, and also published his own newspaper to form opinion.

On August 11th, Antonio Santos and Ti Marto had appeared before him, summoned to come and bring their visionary children with them, Antonio brought Lucia, but Ti Marto independently refused to bring Francisco and Jacinta. The Administrator threatened to take Lucia's life if she did not say what the secret was. Ti Marto expressed himself: "I am here at your orders and I agree with my children." Antonio was still inclined to state his original opinion that everything was a tempest in a teapot, and "just women's talk."

On the morning of the 13th the Administrator came to Aljustrel. Ti Marto has described what happened:

"On the morning of August 13th—it was a Monday—I got a summons to come home from my work at once. Alright, I went. There were a lot of people outside my house, but I was used to that by now. I went inside and was washing my hands. My wife was sitting there. She was nervous and upset and all she did was point to the living room. 'Alright, I'll go in there. Why such a fuss?' So I walked in using a towel, and who should I see but the Mayor himself [i.e., the Administrator]. Even then, I suppose, I wasn't very polite to him, because I saw that a priest was there too, and I went first to shake hands with the priest. Then I said to the Mayor: 'I did not expect to see you here, Sir.' He was a great actor, that man. 'I thought that after all I would like to go to see the miracle today. I thought that we would all go together in my carriage. We will see, and then believe, like St. Thomas,' he said."

When the three children came in together, he offered

them a ride in his carriage. They begged off, but the Administrator said he wanted to stop on the way and see Fr. Ferreira. So the children and their fathers got into the carriage. The Administrator went in to the parish house, and soon called out for Lucia. When he came out shortly with her, before the two men were fully aware of what was happening, he had the children in the carriage and whisked off with them, Francisco in front with him, and Lucia and Jacinta in the back.

"The horse went off at a lively trot,' said Ti Marto. "For awhile it looked as though they were going to the Cova da Iria, but when they got to the main road the horse was whipped suddenly, and they were off, racing toward Ourem, and there was nothing I could do."

The Administrator locked the children in a room of his house and told them they would not leave until they told the secret. Jacinta had a cheerful thought: "If they kill us, it doesn't matter. We'll go straight to heaven." But soon the Administrator's wife came, gave them a lunch and picture books and let them play with her children.

The night of the 13th was strange and lonely, away from home. The next day the Administrator and others coaxed and threatened morning and afternoon. Finally he said he would put them in jail and throw them into a tank of boiling oil. Jacinta began to cry when they reached the jail. "Why do you cry?" Lucia asked. "Because we are going to die without ever again seeing our parents. None of them have come to see us, either yours or mine. They don't care for us anymore. I want to see my mother at least." Francisco suggested that they offer all this for sinners. Jacinta quickly put in more intentions: "Also for the Holy Father and in reparation for offenses against the Immaculate Heart of Mary."

The men in the jail quite naturally tried to comfort the children. One suggested telling the secret. "Be smart, tell the

Mayor the secret and you can go home. It doesn't matter about the Lady." Jacinta looked at the man with amazement: "We'd much rather die than tell the secret." The jail in some ways was a friendly place, especially in these unusual circumstances. One of the prisoners had a concertina. He began to play. An inmate solemnly invited Jacinta to dance. Lucia laughed to see the result as the large man bent over to accommodate the little girl. It was funny, for he didn't have the concertina's quality of compressing itself. So he swept Jacinta up and swept her around the room. But Jacinta soon felt the contrast to the very serious situation and asked the prisoner to put her down. She got a medal from her pocket and hung it on the wall. Then she and the other two children knelt and began to pray the rosary. The prisoners also knelt. One man forgot to take off his hat, and was reminded by Francisco to take it off. He did so, but the amusement of his fellow prisoners made him reassert his independent manhood by throwing the hat forcefully on the floor. Francisco retrieved it and put it on a bench.

Before the prayers were finished a guard came to take the children back to the County House. The Administrator gave elaborate orders in front of the children about having the boiling oil ready. Then he told the children: "It's your last chance to tell the secret. Do you hear?" As he spoke, his eye turned on Jacinta. She was giving signs of fright. "Take that one first. Throw her into the cauldron." The guard led Jacinta out. She fully expected to be boiled alive. The door closed behind her. Francisco told Lucia: "If they kill us, what about it? We'll be in heaven, won't we Lucia? Is there anything more you could want?" He took out his rosary to pray so his little sister should not be afraid. So, next Francisco, and then Lucia were led out separately.

Through the clumsy cleverness of the Administrator, each child had a chance to offer life itself on the altar of fidelity to Our Lady and their own consciences. They just walked into another room, really to meet each other in joyful reunion. But when they were ushered out of the first room, they went with the courage and generosity of young martyrs. To the adults it was a cruel game. To the children, it was real.

There was no bloodshed as far as the children were concerned. There could easily have been real bloodshed and death the other way around. Tempers flared in Fatima on the 13th when it was found out that the children had been abducted. They flared again on the 15th, the feastday of the Assumption, when some young men saw the Administrator. The anger had been such on the 13th and the parish priest was so suspected of being an accomplice of the Administrator, that he found it necessary to deny publicly any complicity in the abduction of the children. Fr. Ferreira sent a letter to the editor of the Catholic paper, *O Mensageiro*: "I refute so unjust as well as insidious a calumny, declaring to everyone that I did not take part in the smallest way, whether directly or indirectly in so odious and sacrilegious an act . . . The calming of the spirits excited by the diabolic rumor was not less providential, otherwise this parish today would mourn the loss of its pastor . . ."

The pastor understood that his life had been in danger. He owed a good bit of the "calming of the excited spirits" to Ti Marto. On the 15th the Administrator also owed his life in all probability to Jacinta and Francisco's father. After the feastday Mass the people were crowding around Ti Marto, asking if he knew where the children were. Reports had them in Santarem. Just then somebody spied the children on the porch of the parish house. Ti Marto does not know how he got there:

"The first thing I knew," he says, "I was holding and hugging my Jacinta. I can even remember that I picked her up and held her in my right arm—so, like this, and I am not ashamed to say my tears were such that they got my little girl all wet. The other two, Francisco and Lucia, they ran up to me. 'Father, Uncle,' they said. 'Give us your blessing.' You can be sure I did, and it was a wonderful moment for me."

Excitement at seeing the children again brought on a resurgence of resentment against their abductor. Fr. Ferreira thought at first Senhor Marto was aiding the tumult. He called as he came to the steps near the children and Ti Marto, "Are you causing all this disturbance?" "Me? I am still holding Jacinta in my arms," replied Ti Marto. "I called down to the people in the square, 'Be quiet, all of you! You are shouting against the Mayor, and you are shouting against Father Ferreira . . . This trouble, I tell you, comes from a lack of faith in God, and that is why He permits it.' " Fr. Ferreira backed up these words, speaking to the people from a window.

The Administrator arrived and showed himself to the people. Ti Marto assured the crowd all was in order; the children were safe. Later the Administrator invited him to have a drink at the tavern. Ti Marto refused, but when he saw young men with cudgels, he decided it best to be seen on a friendly basis with the Administrator. He went along for the glass of wine. The Administrator raised his voice so bystanders could hear: "You can be sure I treated them well."

The children ran to the Cova da Iria. But there was no vision that day.

Chapter Six

St. Joseph Enters

Teresa, sister of Lucia, noticed many colors on the white shirt front of her husband. The air seemed fresher, the sun dim and yellowish. "Maybe we have been wrong all the time," she said to her husband. "Everything's the same as it was six days ago in the Cova." They were along the road from Moita to Fatima. The date was Sunday, August 19 about 4:00 in the afternoon. Lucia, Francisco and John, the older brother of Francisco and Jacinta noticed the same changes in the air and sun. They were at Valinhos, just an open area called by that name, a little distance from Aljustrel. "Hurry and get Jacinta," Lucia urged John. She had just noticed also the flash of lightning that preceded Our Lady's coming. She gave John a few coins as he lingered, hoping to see the vision. He ran finally and found Jacinta.

Not long after Jacinta arrived, Our Lady came. She stood over a holm oak, one a bit taller than the one in the Cova da Iria. "What do you want of me?" Lucia as always was the spokesman. "Come again to the Cova da Iria on the thirteenth of next month, my child, and continue to say the rosary every day." Lucia asked her for some sign, so the people would believe. "In October," the Lady promised, "I will perform a miracle so that everyone can believe in the apparitions. If they had not taken you to the town, the

miracle would be even greater. St. Joseph will come with the
Holy Child to bring peace to the world. Our Lord will come
to bless the people. Our Lady of the Rosary and Our Lady of
Sorrows will also come at that time."

Lucia then asked about what to do with the money the
people left at the Cova. "Two litters should be made; you
and Jacinta are to carry one with two other girls dressed in
white; Francisco is to carry the other with three boys also
dressed in white robes. The money placed on the litters is for
the Feast of Our Lady of the Rosary." Then Lucia asked
about the sick. "Yes, I shall cure some of them within the
year. Pray, pray a great deal and make sacrifices for sinners,
for many souls go to hell for not having someone to pray and
make sacrifices for them." Then the Lady began to rise and
disappeared toward the east as she always did.

Lucia confides that the words about many being lost
because there is no one to pray and make sacrifices for them
had a great effect on her. Jacinta was also preoccupied with
this thought.

As an aftermath of the August appearance, there is a
little sidelight on Jacinta. She and Franciso cut off the
branch on which Our Lady had stood. They stopped at
Lucia's home and Maria Rosa was impressed as were the
others by an indefinable, pleasant odor of the branch. She
decided to keep it, and put the branch on the kitchen table.
Jacinta and Francisco, of course, had intended the branch
for their parents. Later that evening the branch was missing
from the Santos table; Maria, the eldest sister of Lucia, said
they never knew what happened to it. But Ti Marto recalls
Jacinta skipping in the door, looking gay as a bird and
carrying a branch. He could smell the very strong odor. "It is
the branch Our Lady stood on," Jacinta explained. He held
the branch to his nose, but the smell of it had gone.

St. Joseph has a part in the Fatima story. As usual it is a

hidden part. Just as it took a long time for him to be widely noticed in Christian devotion, so not much has been said about him in the half-century since Fatima. But he has a quite definite part in the visions and in the Peace Plan. Our Lady, in fact, made two announcements foretelling his appearance with her and the Child Jesus in October. She said in August and September that he would come in October. Joseph then has a place in three of the six major apparitions. This special attention is not just a case of wifely courtesy.

It indicates that in the Peace Plan, St. Joseph has a special role. Since it is God's plan, it is God who wants Joseph to help in carrying out His divine will. God wants us to give some special attention to St. Joseph. Exactly how St. Joseph's role will develop remains to be seen. We can make some deductions, or at least speculate with some degree of certainty on the nature of his help.

It will be helpful to pay attention to the details of his October appearance. From them an idea may flow, intimating how St. Joseph will help form the cast of mind that is needed to solve the particular problems of the times that hinder the achieving of peace. In the August announcement of St. Joseph's coming, Our Lady had said that he would come with the Child Jesus to give peace to the world. In the September announcement she will use the same words.

It was between the August and September appearances that Lucia found the piece of rope. She tells about it in the second Memoir:

"A couple of days later I found a piece of rope from a cart while taking our flock down the road. I picked it up playfully and tied it to one of my arms. It didn't take me long to find out the rope was hurting me. Then I said to my cousins, 'Look, this causes pain. We can tie it to our waists and offer it to God as a sacrifice.' The poor children accepted my idea right away, and immediately we started to divide it amongst the three of us. Using the edge of a rock and hitting it with another served as a knife. Either because of the thickness or roughness of the rope or because sometimes we tightened it too much, this instrument made us suffer horribly. Sometimes one would see tears on Jacinta's face from the strength of the pain that the rope caused. Several times I told her to take it off, but she said, 'No, I want to offer this sacrifice to Our Lord in reparation, for the conversion of sinners.' "

The Lady would have something to say about the rope on September 13.

A crowd of about 30,000 people came to the Cova da Iria on that date. When the children passed by on the way to the Cova, Lucia recalls that many in the crowd begged cures for the sick in their families, some even kneeling down to implore of them some favor from Our Lady. "They asked to have their sons and husbands brought back from the war. They asked for the conversion of some particular sinner. They asked for the cure of consumption. They asked for everything. Every ailment of humanity seemed to be paraded before us." There were also those who scoffed and made crude jokes. Jacinta, used to tender acceptance at home, always found the scoffers a painful trial. In the Cova many prayed the rosary.

From a place higher up in the rough amphitheatre of the Cova and at some distance from the place where the children awaited their Lady were two priests. One was Monsignor John Quaresma, vicar-general of the diocese. He had an open mind. Most priests had adverse opinions or were quite skeptical about the Fatima events that had stirred up the country and brought out this large crowd. Priests were one of the children's biggest, involuntary penances. "They kept questioning us and questioning us, and then, as if that were not enough, they would start all over, from the very beginning," says Lucia in Memoir II. This was going on and picking up momentum through the gathering interest of the summer days. "Whenever we saw a priest coming, we did our best to escape, and when we were caught and had to oblige them, we offered it to God as one of our greatest sacrifices."

Monsignor John Quaresma kept at a quiet distance. He tells what happened on September 13:

"At midday there was complete silence. One only heard the murmur of prayers. Suddenly there were sounds of jubilation and voices praising the Blessed Virgin. Arms were raised pointing to something in the sky. 'Look, don't you see? Yes, yes, I do . . .' There had not been a cloud in the deep blue of the sky, and I too raised my eyes and scrutinized it in case I should be able to distinguish what the others, more fortunate than I, had already claimed to have seen. With great astonishment I saw, clearly and distinctly, a luminous globe, which moved from the east to the west, gliding slowly and majestically through space. My friend also looked, and had the good fortune to enjoy the same unexpected and delightful vision. Suddenly the globe, with its extraordinary light disappeared. Near us was a little girl dressed like Lucia and more or less the same age. She continued to cry out happily: 'I still see it. I still see it! Now it's coming down . . . !' "

The little girl gave an excited description again as she saw the globe moving back up and away to the east. Monsignor asked his fellow priest: "What do you think of that globe?" "That it was Our Lady," he answered without hesitation. There was an air of joy and jubilation. Some saw nothing. An old lady cried bitterly because she had seen nothing. Others noted signs similar to those that happened at earlier visions: a paling of the sun till stars were visible, a falling of petals that disappeared like snow melting before it touches the ground. There was a sudden freshening of the air.

"What do you want of me?" people near Lucia heard her ask. Anybody could hear her half of the conversation. Just she and Jacinta heard the other half. Francisco too did not hear, but he saw the Lady.

"Let the people continue to say the rosary every day to obtain the end of the war. In the last month, in October, I shall perform a miracle so that all may believe in my apparitions. If they had not taken you to the town the miracle would have been greater. St. Joseph will come with the Baby Jesus to give peace to the world. Our Lord also will come to bless the people. Besides, Our Lady of the Rosary and Our Lady of Sorrows will come."

From the promise of a cosmic miracle for the people and the apparitional presence of St. Joseph and the Child Jesus and Christ as an adult, Our Lady descended to a little personal secret of the children. "God is pleased with your sacrifices, but does not wish that you sleep with the rope. Wear it only during the day." Mary had given the children a secret. They had some of their own, and chief of these were their many sacrifices. They tried to keep these under cover so they would not be prohibited from doing them, and also from natural reticence about such matters. It is of much interest that the Blessed Virgin did not tell these young children to put aside the rope altogether.

Lucia asked Our Lady about the multitude of cures. "In the course of the year she will be improved," Mary said of a deaf-mute girl. Of the others, "Some I will cure; but the others, no. Our Lord does not have confidence in them." Lucia then said that the people would like to have a chapel built. "Use half of the money received so far for the litters. On one of them, place the statue of Our Lady of the Rosary.

The other half should be set aside to help with the building of the chapel."

Moses committed a fault by striking the rock twice, to get water. Lucia, with a child's need and oppressed by accusations and reproofs, committed no fault. She asked after hearing Mary's promise two times: "Many say I am a swindler who should be hanged or burned. Please perform a miracle for all to believe." The reassurance came: "Yes, in October, I will perform a miracle so that all may believe." "Some people gave me these two letters for you, and a bottle of cologne," Lucia offered. "None of that is necessary for heaven." Our Lady began to leave, going toward the east. People looking in that direction as Lucia shouted and pointed, saw the luminous globe moving away and rising.

In the second Memoir, Lucia comments about the rope: "Needless to say, we readily obeyed her orders." This agreeable combination of generosity with obedience finds frequent application in the lives of the children. They found guidance from several priests of kindly disposition. One was Fr. Francisco da Cruz of Lisbon, and another was Fr. Faustino Ferreira, whom Lucia always speaks of as the pastor of Olival, perhaps because his family name is the same as that of the pastor of Fatima. They suggested practices of piety and explained how to answer some questions without lying or revealing the Blessed Virgin's secret, and helped moderate the penances.

As the great day of the promised October miracle drew near, the pressures on the children and their families increased. Maria dos Anjos, Lucia's oldest sister gives some insight on this:

"The closer the day came, the more we insisted that she give up this dream of hers. We would all have to suffer because of her imaginings. Father scolded her often, though he never struck her. Mother was not so easy. One rumor was going around that they would place bombs at the Cova da Iria to scare everyone that went there. Some people suggested that mother lock the children in a room until they denied the whole story. We did not speak of it in front of Lucia, but we were frightened and we wondered what was going to happen to us. Some others suggested that we take Lucia away some place where no one could find her. We didn't know what to do."

"If it were Our Lady, she could have performed a miracle already, started a spring or something else," Lucia's mother lamented. "O how will this all end?"

Maria continues:

"But the children showed no fear at all. I went to the children one day as they were speaking at the well. 'Have you decided yet that you saw nothing? They are warning us that they will throw bombs at our homes.'" Maria offered to take their denial to the pastor. Jacinta, with tears in her eyes, said softly, "Yes, you may do as you wish, but we have seen."

Jacinta and Francisco had it much better at home. Their father, Ti Marto, supported them. He believed they were telling the truth, and he had a supreme confidence in the providence of God. A priest from a neighboring parish stopped in early October to throw all his weight into forcing the children to admit they had been lying. When he mentioned witchcraft, Ti Marto became very angry, and Jacinta left quickly, for she hated to see anger displayed. This happened away from the home, where the priest had found them. When the group came to the Marto home, Jacinta was sitting outside combing another little girl's hair. The priest's companion offered Jacinta a coin. Ti Marto turned his hand back. The priest told her that Lucia had told all. "No, Lucia told nothing," Jacinta replied.

Many newspapers in Portugal sent reporters to cover the events of October 13. Descriptions of how the throng of

70,000 (some estimates are higher) converged on the Cova da Iria are colorful and graphic. *O Dia* of Lisbon reported:

"For days prior to the thirteenth, groups of pilgrims traveled toward Fatima. They came on foot, buskins on their brawny legs, food bags on their heads, across the pine groves, where the crowberries seem like drops of dew upon the verdure, along the sands where the windmills rotate. A slow and swaying gait swung the hems of their skirts from side to side and waved orange kerchiefs upon which sat their black hats . . . People from everywhere whom the voice of the miracle had reached, left their homes and fields, and came on foot, by horse or by carriage. They traveled the highways and the roads, between hills and pine groves. For two days these came to life with the rolling of the carriages, the trot of the donkeys and the voices of the pilgrims . . . Water dripped from the caps and broad-rimmed hats onto the new jackets of their suits for seeing God. The bare feet of the women and the hobnailed shoes of the men sloshed in the wide pools of the muddy roads. They seemed not to notice the rain . . . A murmur drifting down from the hills reached us. It was a murmur like the distant voice of the sea lowered faintly before the silence of the fields. It was the religious songs, now becoming clear, intoned by thousands of voices. Over the plateau, over a hill, or filling a valley, there was a wide and shuffling mass of thousands upon thousands of souls in prayer."

Even Lucia's mother decided to go. "If my daughter dies, I want to be at her side." Lucia embraced her mother: "Don't fear, for nothing will happen to us. Our Lady shall do what she promised." Ti Marto reassured his wife, Olympia, as people crowded into their home, dragging in mud, even standing on the beds. "Don't let it bother you. When the house is full no one else can come in." Last minute warnings about danger came from priests and friends. "Look, if they hurt us, we'll go to heaven," said Jacinta. "Pity them, for they shall go to hell."

Near the holm oak a big man, a chauffeur, picked up Jacinta and carried her, setting her down close to the once leafy pedestal of Mary. The crush there was so great that Jacinta began to cry. Lucia and Francisco placed her between them. A priest hostile to the whole idea, pulled out his watch and told the people: "Everyone out of here. The whole thing is an illusion." He tried to push the children away. Lucia, near tears, said: "Whoever wants to go, may go. I'm not going. I'm on my own property." Just then the flash came and Lucia said, "Jacinta, kneel down. Our Lady is coming. I've seen the flash." The Lady's feet touched the flowery decorations atop the stump of the holm oak. "What do you want of me?" Lucia asked. In this final visit she was again the spokesman. Once Maria de Capelinha asked why Our Lady spoke only with Lucia. "It's because Jacinta is tongue-tied. If she would only speak to Our Lady, I know Our Lady would speak to her," Lucia answered. Jacinta, standing nearby, just looked at them and smiled. Her little world had its precisions. She just listened again as Our Lady gave her short October message.

"I want to tell you to have them build a chapel here in my honor. I am the Lady of the Rosary. Let them continue to say the rosary every day. The war is going to end, and the soldiers will soon return to their homes." Lucia asked for the cures and conversions people had begged. Our Lady replied, "Some, yes, others, no. It is necessary that they amend their lives and ask pardon for their sins." Then as Lucia tells it in the fourth Memoir: "Her face became grave as she continued: 'Let them offend Our Lord no more, for He is already much offended.' And opening her hands she made the light emerging from them ascend to where the sun ought to be. And while she was arising, her own radiance continued shining towards the sun."

This the children saw. It was the moment for the miracle of the sun the people saw in the Cova and in a radius of 30 miles. The poet, Alfonso Lopes Vieira, working at noon on the veranda of his home in San Pedro de Muel, saw the phenomenon and in surprise called for his wife and her mother to come and see. This was 30 miles from the Cova. At Alburitel, nine miles from Fatima, the school teacher, Senhora Delfina Pereira Lopes, ran with the children into the street. There, others prayed and shouted and cried, thinking the world was coming to an end. The Baron of Alvaiazere, an attorney of Ourem, had come to the Cova for diversion. He was braced against the force of collective suggestion. He later wrote: "I knew it was necessary to be on my guard, not to allow myself to be influenced. I only know that I shouted, 'I believe, I believe, I believe' and that tears fell from my eyes, wondering, ecstatic before this manifestation of divine power."

All who saw did not convert. Avelino de Almeida had written the *O Seculo* article in an objective manner, stating what others described they saw. A friend wrote and put the question to Almeida: "What did you see?" Almeida answered his friend, Antonio de Bastos of Santarem, like himself a one-time Catholic, now a rationalist. He wrote a piece for *Illustracao Portuguesa*, entitled: "Letter to Someone Who Asks For an Objective Testimony." Almeida wrote:

"You were a believer in your youth and later ceased to be one . . . Your rationalism suffered a formidable blow [at Fatima, October 13] . . . And now when I could not imagine seeing anything more impressive than this rumor-filled but peaceful crowd . . . what did I now see of real uniqueness in the plain of Fatima? The rain stops falling at the foretold hour, the thick mass of clouds is broken, and the sun—a disk of smoky silver—appears at full zenith and begins to dance in a violent and convulsive dance . . . very beautiful and shining colors successively pass over the face of the sun. Miracle, as the people shouted; natural phenomenon, as the learned say! I now don't care to know, but only to tell you what I saw . . . The rest is with Science and the Church."

As the thousands of people—mostly receptive, some scoffing, some quietly rationalistic like Almeida, some violently opposed—watched the beginning of the miracle of the sun, the three children also looked toward the sun. As Lucia wrote in her Memoir, "Here you have, Your Excellency, the reason why I shouted that they should look at the sun. My purpose was not to bring the attention of the crowd to the sun, because I didn't notice them. I was not even aware of their presence. I did so, moved by an inner force which impelled me to act thus."

"When Our Lady disappeared in the immense distance of the sky, next to the sun we saw St. Joseph holding the Child Jesus and Our Lady dressed in white with a blue mantle. St. Joseph and the Child seemed to be blessing the world, making the sign of the cross. Shortly after this vision had vanished, I saw Our Lord and Our Lady who reminded me of Our Lady of Sorrows. Our Lord was blessing the world just the same way as St. Joseph. This vision vanished too, and it seemed to me I again saw Our Lady in a form resembling that of Our Lady of Mt. Carmel."

We can note that Lucia goes from the plural "we saw" to the singular "I saw" for the final two visions near the sun. Fr. Luis Gonzaga da Fonseca, S.J. states: "Like Lucia, her cousins had seen the Holy Family for a few minutes, but not the other visions." Since Lucia herself was asked to and suggested corrections for his book, it seems that Francisco and Jacinta saw the Holy Family, but not Our Lady of

Sorrows and the Lord, nor Our Lady of Mt. Carmel. The way Jacinta answered the questions of Fr. Formigao on October 13 and 19 also shows the validity of this conclusion. "Was the Child standing or being carried?" Jacinta said, "He was standing." Lucia's answer had been, "He was being carried." In answer to the question, "Did you see St. Joseph," Jacinta replied, "Yes, Lucia said that St. Joseph gave a blessing." It seems that only Lucia saw St. Joseph holding the Child and together with Him blessing the world. Both were dressed in red according to Lucia and Jacinta. They are more definite on the color of St. Joseph's garments than on those of Jesus. All three children also saw the signs in the sun. Jacinta answered Fr. Formigao's question about this by saying, "I turned my eyes to the side." This answer indicates that the solar prodigy seen by the thousands and the visions near the sun seen by the children were at least in part simultaneous. The positions of the Holy Family were: Joseph, Jesus and Mary from left to right as they stood. No words were spoken by any member of the Holy Family apparition.

Antonio, Lucia's father let go her hand in the course of the rush and pressure of the crowd. Dr. Carlos Mendes carried her for awhile on top of his shoulder, and she exhorted the crowd to do penance. For awhile she was not to be found, going from group to group. That evening, she noticed that her long hair had been snipped off. From the events of that day and some days following of questionings and excitement, the children were left exhausted.

After two announcements in August and September, St. Joseph came to Fatima at its greatest moment. He came as the miracle of the sun began. He came just after Our Lady had completed her promised six visits to the Cova. With him was the Child Jesus as an infant of one or two years of age. With him was Our Lady, now dressed in white with a blue mantle, Our Lady of the Rosary. All these circumstances point to a role of great importance for St. Joseph in God's Peace Plan. Nothing was said. Perhaps this indicates a quiet, behind-the-scenes, hidden role. Since it is God's will that peace come through the Immaculate Heart of Mary, St. Joseph's part must have a close connection with the greater honoring and understanding of her Heart. Since Joseph comes with the Child, "to bring peace to the world," we will find our clues to what God wants in the Holy Family while Jesus was a child. Since Mary appeared with Jesus and Joseph in the garb of Our Lady of the Rosary, and since her constant message was to pray the rosary, and she gave this as her title, we know that St. Joseph's part in bringing peace will also be connected with the rosary.

In the way divine providence works, the achievement of this needs the help of St. Joseph, not only as intercessor, but as model for husbands and fathers. The love of Joseph for the Immaculate Heart, her love for him, their mutual love for the Child, all converge to throw light on the dynamics that bring peace. (For more on this, see Appendix C.)

Chapter Seven

The Way to be a Giant

After the great 13th in October of 1917, the life of Jacinta falls into two periods. The same may be said for Francisco. The first period lasted a year. It was a time of trying to get back to normal living, but attended by the inevitable afterflow of the vision events as they affected other people.

After the great 13th, many came to believe, and they held the little shepherd children in reverence, almost as uncanonized saints. They besieged them, asking for their prayers. Many who did not believe continued to harass and ridicule them. One woman beat up Lucia. The papers left innuendos about other condemned visionaries. Complaint was made about the money left for a chapel, when this did not materialize soon enough. Maria de Capelinha had charge of this money, with the approval of the pastor, and the pastor did so under direction of the Archbishop of Lisbon.

The chapel was held up because Fr. Ferreira did not see much reason to encourage it. He was repairing the church, and saw little reason to put a chapel out in the country. His own treatment of the children is a strange mixture of kindness and lack of acceptance. Probably he just did not know what to do. The whole world, it seemed, had descended on his peaceful little parish. We must remember that his own life had been endangered, and he felt the live, raw emotion of the haters and read the harsh criticisms. The answer to his state of mind lies essentially in his own conflict. He was buffeted by friends among the clergy both ways. Had his own convictions about the events been firm, his conflict would have been less, and it would have been easier for the children. Eventually he resigned, and this brought down the wrath of some parishioners on the children, especially Lucia. She felt things so keenly, that one day she threw up to Jacinta the fact that if she had only kept quiet from the beginning, nobody would ever have known anything. Jacinta, as she had done before, begged her pardon with tears. Lucia also had the frightening experience of being cornered by cavalrymen sent to put a stop to people holding gatherings at the Cova. The two cavalrymen made her walk between their horses down the road. Once they stopped and suggested cutting off her head, burying her and so ending all the trouble. Lucia thought it was her last hour.

Both families eventually had to sell their flocks because of the many troubles caused by the visions. Besides the land being trampled down, there was also the time taken up by the children's constantly being questioned. Endlessly the visitors sought them out, to ask all kinds of questions. They became adept in hiding—up in a tree, under the bed, away down the road. One day they saw some gentlemen and ladies getting out of an auto. They could not go unseen. When asked, they gave precise directions on how to get to their houses, then ran to hide in a patch of brambles. Jacinta said: "We must always do this whenever we are not known."

The ones they ran away from the most gladly were priests. This was one point that Fr. Ferreira had against them. He wanted to oblige the priests who stopped at the rectory; perhaps, endlessly searching himself to make sense out of everything, he was hoping for some unexpected light the priests' questions might bring. None of the stream of clergy or others of long forensic training could trip them up, or find any contradictions in their stories. Nor could anything be found that would run counter to good theology or to the Church's teaching. In the meantime, the children, wiser than those who questioned, offered to Jesus and Mary the sacrifice it meant to them. They would much have preferred to be out with the sheep, or praying or playing.

For awhile the three children went to school. A school for girls had opened about that time in Fatima. Lucia had not learned to read, but had been drilled by oral instruction in the catechism. She had even been allowed to make her first Communion before the usual age of 10. She had a new reason for going to school, since the Blessed Virgin herself had told her to learn to read and write. After the flocks were sold, there was no good excuse for staying away from school. Francisco was somewhat of a truant. The teacher did not think him much of a scholar when he was there. He much preferred to go to St. Anthony's Church and sit quietly, thinking and praying his rosary. He had one reason for not going to school which was unique. He expected to die before long. "Why don't you study?" His answer in so many words was: "What's the use? I'll soon be going to heaven."

The children had several good reasons for not wanting to be questioned again and again. It took much time and was fatiguing. They also did not want their penitential practices to be known, and since offering sacrifices was one of Our Lady's repeated pieces of advice, a follow-up question about that must have been quite natural: "Are you doing any penances?" Some questioners were also tricky and devious, trying to catch them up. Again they feared that in answering they might either tell a lie or reveal the Lady's secrets.

It was especially on the perplexities of this dilemma that

several priests helped them very much. Fr. Cruz of Lisbon and the pastor of Olival, Fr. Faustino Ferreira helped to guide them. Jacinta picked up a favorite prayer from Fr. Cruz: "Sweet Heart of Mary, be my salvation." She made up a little tune which she sang at times while gathering flowers: "Sweet Heart of Mary, be my salvation. Immaculate Heart of Mary, convert sinners, save souls from hell." Lucia considers Fr. Faustino her first spiritual director. It was Fr. Formigao who first taught Lucia to thank God for all the special graces He was giving her. "My God I love You, thank You for the graces you have granted me." This became a favorite practice with Jacinta. Lucia says in Memoir II: "In the middle of the most distracting games she would ask: 'Have you forgotten to thank Our Lord for the graces He has given to us?' " Fr. Formigao also told Lucia about St. Agnes, and encouraged her to imitate the young martyr virgin. As the children talked together about their deep experiences, they helped one another gradually to fill in and make more solid their spiritual life. They shared the advice given them by these various priests.

The fact that when they could, they avoided questioning does not mean that they were uncooperative. In an arranged interview or when they chanced to be caught (as happened over and over) they were very polite, and answered truthfully to the point of near-scrupulosity. Lucia says that Jacinta was shy, and was afraid of saying more than she should. "As Jacinta, when questioned, used to hang her head, look at the ground and not say hardly a word, I was called on most of the time to satisfy the curiosity of pilgrims." Jacinta opened up only when the person inspired in her a feeling of confidence. If pressed too hard, Jacinta could grow a bit confused. She then referred the person to Lucia.

The pastor one day asked Lucia a hard question: "Why

do all these people prostrate themselves on a waste piece of land, and leave the living God of our altars alone and abandoned in the tabernacle?" She had no answer, and regretted that she could do nothing. "Had I been the master of all those people's hearts, I would certainly have driven them to church."

The second part of Jacinta's life after the visions, began in the fall of 1918. The worldwide influenza epidemic struck the Marto and Santos families. Ti Marto and Lucia were the only ones who escaped it. For Francisco and Jacinta this was the beginning of the drawn-out complications which led to their deaths. School days were over. They had barely started before they graduated into the hard school of the cross. It would test them to the last breath. In generosity and courage, they would both get an A plus.

Francisco went to confession shortly before he died. He sent Lucia to ask Jacinta if she knew anything he should confess. Her sisterly memory brought out, after a few moments of thought: "Before Our Lady appeared to us, he stole a tostao [a small coin] from his father to buy the mouth-organ of Jose Marto from Casa Velha, and that when the boys of Aljustrel threw stones at Boleiros he also threw some." Francisco said he had confessed that, but would again. When Lucia earlier asked him to remember in heaven to pray for "sinners, for the Holy Father, for me and Jacinta," he said: "Yes, I will, but look, ask Jacinta these things instead. I am afraid I will forget them when I see Our Lord. First I want to console Him." When Lucia wrote this in 1941, she reflected: "And now I append, probably he didn't! Patience!" Lucia was with him the night before he died, and asked again: "Don't forget me in heaven." This time he promised: "I won't forget you, no. Don't worry." As both Francisco and Lucia were crying and clasping hands, Olympia told Lucia to go to another room. She left saying: "Good-bye Francisco, good-bye till heaven."

Francisco made his first and only Communion the day before he died. The pastor brought him Viaticum. He tried to sit up, but was too weak. As he had so often done in the past two years, he offered everything to comfort the Hearts of Jesus and Mary. That evening he spoke up suddenly: "Look, what a beautiful light, by the door. Now it's gone. I can't see it any more." Jacinta had said just a few days earlier, that Our Lady had told her she was coming for Francisco in a very short time. Perhaps that evening she had opened the door of heaven a little to look out and smile a welcome. Tomorrow she would open it wide. Francisco died peacefully about ten in the morning, April 4, 1919. They carried the casket the next day, a Saturday, to the parish cemetery. Jacinta was too sick to go. For the rest of her short life, she had a new sacrifice to offer the Hearts of Jesus and Mary. She missed Francisco very much. One of her last instructions to him was: "Give my best wishes, my very best wishes to Our Lord and Our Lady. Tell them I'll suffer all they want me to, for the conversion of sinners, and in reparation for the sins committed against the Immaculate Heart of Mary." *I'll suffer all they want me to* is a brave offer. Jacinta had 10½ months to write in tears and blood the response of Jesus and Mary in accepting her generous offer.

Jacinta was not in bed all this time, nor confined to the house. When she could she went to church, or to the Cova, or to the Cabezo, or to Lucia's house. She was moved to Francisco's room. Sometimes children came in and she sat on the floor with them and played games. But gradually her health weakened. At times she sat up in bed for hours, and the sadness of her face prompted questions about what her thoughts were. To Lucia she confided that she missed Francisco very much. Often she answered the same question of Lucia: "Of that war which is coming, of the many people who are going to die and go to hell. What a shame. If they would stop offending God, neither the war would come nor would they go to hell." Jacinta spoke with certainty about a coming war. Once she told Lucia: "Don't be afraid when the war starts. In heaven I will be praying for you."

She mentioned the strange light that was to be a signal announcing World War II. ". . . When, some night you see the light that Our Lady told us would come, you run away and go to heaven too." "Don't you see that nobody can run away and go to heaven?" Jacinta replied, "That's right, you can't. But don't be afraid. In heaven I will pray a great deal for you, for the Holy Father, for Portugal so the war won't come here, and for all priests." (Memoir III)

Jacinta, the quiet one, did not say even to her closest confidante, Lucia, "Well, today Our Lady told me . . ." Mary did keep in close touch with Jacinta, but when Jacinta mentioned anything, it came out as part of a conversation. She did not introduce it. She knew a long time ahead that she would go to two hospitals but not be cured. Lucia gives this information in a postscript to her second Memoir. "I forgot to say that when Jacinta was taken to the hospitals of Vila Nova de Ourem and Lisbon, she knew she was not going to be healed but to suffer. A long time before anyone had spoken about her going into the hospital of Vila Nova de Ourem she said one day, 'Our Lady wants me to go to two hospitals. But it is not to be cured. It is to suffer more for the love of Our Lord and for sinners.'"

Ti Marto took his daughter by donkey to St. Augustin Hospital in Ourem. Her mother and Lucia came to visit her several times. She stayed in the hospital for two months in the summer of 1919. The treatment was very painful and useless in effecting any improvement. She returned home worse than when she left, with a large wound in her left side which drained constantly and had to be dressed daily. Fr.

Formigao visited her after her return from Ourem and was shocked. He wrote: "Jacinta is like a skeleton and her arms are shockingly thin. Since she left the local hospital where she underwent two months of useless treatment, the fever has never left her. She looks pathetic. Tuberculosis, after an attack of bronchial pneumonia and purulent pleurisy is undermining her enfeebled constitution. Only careful treatment in a good sanatorium can save her. But her parents cannot undertake the expense which such a treatment involves."

Jacinta still tried to say the angel's prayer, getting out of bed and bowing to the ground, but she toppled over, trying to bow. She confided this to Lucia. In turn Lucia told it to Fr. Faustino Jacinto Ferreira, pastor of Olival. He advised that Jacinta say her prayers in bed. Jacinta was doubtful about whether this would be just what God wanted, but when reassured by Lucia, she followed the good priest's suggestion.

Jacinta persuaded her mother to take her once more to the Cova. Her mother and a friend took her on the donkey. Jacinta could hardly stand. She picked a few flowers for the primitive altar of the chapel and prayed. Leave-taking was hard on Jacinta, whether from a loved place or a loved face. During her stay in the hospital at Ourem her pains were many. But her separation from family and Lucia was the biggest sacrifice of all. The Blessed Virgin had told her that she would go to another hospital, and also by this time had specified that it would be Lisbon. There she would die, separated from family and Lucia. She told Lucia: "I shall go to Lisbon, to another hospital. I shan't see you nor my parents again. When I have suffered a great deal, I shall die alone, but I mustn't be afraid, because she will come to take me to heaven." She wept and embraced Lucia: "I shall never see you again. You won't come to see me. O pray much for me, for I shall die all alone. . . ."

Lucia told her one day not to think about dying alone. This was the thought that hurt her most. Jacinta responded: "Let me think about it. The more I think, the more I suffer and I want to suffer for love of Our Lord and for sinners. What does it matter after all? Our Lady is coming to take me to heaven." Once in awhile she hugged her crucifix, kissed it and said: "Oh Jesus, I love You and I want to suffer a great deal for love of You." Again she said: "Oh Jesus, now You can convert many sinners because this sacrifice is such a big one." Another time she would say: "Am I going to die without receiving the hidden Jesus? If only Our Lady would bring Him to me, when she comes to take me to heaven."

One of Jacinta's trials was that she could not receive Holy Communion. She had not reached the customary age, and no exception was made for her. Lucia had received earlier than usual because of her exceptional mastery of the catechism. In the case of Francisco and Jacinta, so favored and so sick, we might wonder if the point was not over-emphasized, perhaps just because they were already exceptions. Jacinta often asked Lucia to come on the way home from church after receiving Communion, so she could rejoice in the thought of how close the *hidden Jesus* was. Jacinta and Francisco usually used this way of speaking about Jesus in the Holy Eucharist.

In these last months, the recurrent thought of Jacinta was that she would die alone. Her words on one occasion bring back the words spoken in a garden: "Father, if it is possible, let this chalice pass from me" (Mt 26:39). Lucia describes the occasion in Memoir I.

"One day I found her embracing a picture of Our Lady while she said: 'Oh my beloved heavenly Mother, must I really die alone?' The poor little child was very upset at the thought of having to die alone. In order to encourage her, I said, 'What does it matter, dying alone, if Our Lady comes for you?' 'It is true, it doesn't matter, but I don't know why, sometimes I forget that she is coming to fetch me. I only think of how I shall die without you being near me.' "

Even after her return from St. Augustin Hospital, Jacinta was able at times to go to Mass. On her return, her strength would be so drained that she just fell on the bed. Lucia told her she should not go, because it was not a Sunday, but Jacinta said: "It doesn't matter. I will go for sinners who don't go even on Sundays." When she heard loud cursing, she covered her face with her hands, and said: "Oh, my God, don't these people realize that this kind of talk might send them to hell? Forgive them, Jesus and convert them. They certainly don't know they are offending God. Oh, what a pity. Jesus, I will pray for them." She would also at times, come right out and say to somebody not to do what might offend God. More often, the policy for her and Francisco was to take flight and avoid what might develop into a situation they thought offended God.

In mid-January of 1920 a doctor from Lisbon and his wife stopped by to see Jacinta. He was Dr. Eurico Lisboa, an opthamologist. He was shocked by her appearance. "She was thin and pale and walked with great difficulty," he wrote. He got in touch with Fr. Formigao and with his aid persuaded the family to send Jacinta to the hospital in Lisbon. They did not have the money, but he agreed to arrange for a good surgeon to take care of Jacinta.

Her mother and oldest brother, Antonio took her on the train. Olympia was advised to keep a window open because of the bad odor of Jacinta's suppurating wound. Jacinta sat or stood by the window, getting her first look at the world beyond the little radius of a day's travel by donkey. She took much interest in the people and the countryside. When they arrived in Lisbon, several ladies identified Antonio by a pre-arranged handkerchief tied to his wrist. But the well-to-do family that was to receive Jacinta as a guest, refused on seeing her condition. They went to several institutions, but nobody would make an arrangement to take Jacinta in. A picture floats into memory again of a scene in the life of Jesus, Mary and Joseph. There was no room in the inn.

A small orphanage, run by a Franciscan tertiary, Mother Maria Purificao Godinho, welcomed Jacinta. There were about twenty children there. Mother Godinho was affectionately called *Madrinha* or godmother. Olympia stayed about a week with Jacinta and then returned to Aljustrel. A lady who met them in the waiting room of the orphanage, gave a fifty escudo note to Jacinta. She turned it over to Mother Godinho to pay for her keep. Jacinta soon was calling the kindly nun, *Madrinha* and also called the orphanage "Our Lady of Fatima's House."

Her two weeks spent here were made pleasant by the Madrinha's care and company. Mother Godinho was a believer in Fatima, and had prayed for the favor of getting to know the children. There was a chapel in the orphanage and the Blessed Sacrament was reserved. Jacinta used to go and spend a long time sitting and looking at the tabernacle. Jacinta sat on a chair in the choir. Before her mother left, she asked to be taken to confession. After her confession at the neighboring church, she was radiantly happy. "What a good priest that was," she told Olympia. "He asked me so many things." Olympia, reporting this said: "I keep saying to myself how much I would give to know what the good Father had asked her, to give her this happiness, but of course it is not anyone else's business what happens in confession."

Jacinta was friendly with the other children, but especially liked to be with one little girl about her age. Mother Godinho had some very inspirational eavesdropping as Jacinta explained to her new friend: "You must not lie or be lazy or disobedient, and you must bear everything with patience for love of Our Lord, if you want to go to heaven."

In the orphanage and at the hospital, Jacinta had visits from Our Lady, perhaps also from St. Joseph and her guardian angel. One day, when Mother Godinho came to see her, Jacinta asked her to come later: "Come later, godmother. I am waiting now for the Blessed Virgin." Jacinta's deeply mystical soul invited God's special favors. Besides the understanding of greater mysteries, these visits brought her a gift of knowing other details. When Mother Godinho expressed a hope of one day going to the Cova, Jacinta assured her that she would go soon. It happened just that way, and Mother Godinho was assigned by her superiors to accompany Jacinta's body on the train. Jacinta also dictated a letter to Lucia, in which she told her that Our Lady had appeared and revealed the day and hour of her death.

When Mother Godinho took Jacinta to the hospital Dona Estefania, she came in for a scolding from the doctors and nurses for not bringing the child sooner. Dr. Lisboa was in charge of these arrangements, and Jacinta would have much preferred to die at the orphanage. She said that the operation would be useless. Her diagnosis was "purulent pleurisy of the large left cavity, fistulous osteitis of the seventh and eighth ribs of the same side." "Purulent pleurisy" means that her chest membrane was inflamed and discharging pus; "fistulous osteitis" means that the bones were inflamed and that an abcess had formed.

Because of her weakened condition, no general anaesthetic was given. She was awake during the operation, under local anaesthesia. Her delicate sense of modesty made her cry bitterly when her clothing was taken from her. Dr. Leonardo de Castro Freire, assisted by Dr. Elvas operated on February 10. He was chief surgeon of the hospital and a child specialist. He cut away two ribs on the left side, leaving an opening large enough to put his hand in. During the operation and in the very painful days that followed, she repeated, "O my good Mother, O my good Mother." Sometimes she reminded herself out loud: "Patience, we must all suffer to get to heaven." Her father had come to see her once, but had hurried home where at the time he was needed because other children were sick.

On February 16 she had exceptionally severe and sharp pains. But the next day she told Mother Godinho who came to see her: "Our Lady appeared to me again. She will soon come for me. She has taken away all my pain."

In Memoir III Lucia writes: "Sometimes I have been asked if Our Lady in any apparition, had pointed out what kind of sins offend God the most, because they say Jacinta when in Lisbon had designated the sins of the flesh. She often questioned me about this particular thing; perhaps in Lisbon she decided to question Our Lady herself and this was the answer she received." According to the book, *Our Lady of Light* by Berthas-DaFonseca Our Lady made this revelation to Jacinta when she came to her and took away her pains in the hospital at Lisbon a few days before she died. Jacinta, after telling Mother Godinho that her pains were taken away, added that this time the Blessed Virgin looked very sad, and had told her why. "The sins which lead the greatest number of souls to perdition are the sins of the flesh. Luxurious living must be avoided, people must do penance and repent of their sins. Great penance is indispensable."

Dr. Lisboa noted that about this time Jacinta was again able to enjoy distractions and to play. "She liked to look at holy pictures," he said, "one among them in particular—given me later as a souvenir—of Our Lady of Sameiro, which she said most closely resembled the Lady of the Apparitions. I was told several times that Jacinta wished to see me, but as my professional duties were heavy and Jacinta was apparently better, I unfortunately put off my visit until too late."

Fr. Pereira dos Reis of the Church of the Holy Angels came and heard her confession on the evening of February 20, as she said about 6 o'clock that she was going to die. He promised to bring her Communion the next day, thinking she looked quite well, or at least not in immediate danger. She said it would be too late. She was right. She did not receive Viaticum.

The nurse in attendance in the children's section was Aurora Gomez. "Aurora" means "dawn." William Walsh describes in touching words the death of her little patient. "At 10:30 that evening the nurse left her for a few moments, and returned just in time to see her breathe her last sigh, a rosy flush on her cheeks, a half smile on her lips. It was night in the dingy hospital, but it was forever dawn in the soul of Jacinta, as the Mother of God bent over bed 60 and gathered her into the arms that had enfolded the Christ in infancy and in death."

It was the Friday before Ash Wednesday, February 20, 1920. Jacinta would have been 10 on her next birthday, March 11th. Word had been sent to Jacinta's family that after the operation she was doing well. Ti Marto and Olympia were relieved, and continued in caring for the sick at home. News of her death reached them in a kindly way. Ti Marto was asked by letter to go to Ourem at once to see the Baron Alvaiazere. When he arrived there, he was given something to eat, and then the Baron handed him a letter.

His little girl was dead. Ti Marto had to go home and break the news to the family.

In Lisbon, Dr. Lisboa took charge of the arrangements. One of his patients, Dona Amelia Castro got a white First Communion dress and a blue sash. It had been used in the family. Jacinta was laid out as she had wished, in Our Lady's colors. The first plan was for her to be buried in Lisbon. But Dr. Lisboa reconsidered, and made arrangements for her body to go to Ourem, and be placed in the burial vault of the Baron Alvaiazere. While these negotiations were going on, the body was taken to the parish church of the Holy Angels. The pastor, Fr. Reis, was against this, but Dr. Lisboa and others were good persuaders. Fr. Reis was worried about premature veneration and also about health rules. In Portugal the rule was for burial to be within 24 hours of death. The body rested humbly in its little coffin on two stools in a corner of the sacristy.

Fr. Reis was right about the signs of veneration. In the hospital, Jacinta had been hardly noticed. She was one of the patients, had very few visitors, made no disturbance. Probably only the immediately concerned people knew she was one of the Fatima children. After she died, word got around, and a stream of pilgrims began to flow. They touched rosaries, medals and statues to Jacinta's dress and prayed. Fr. Reis grew more apprehensive. He handed the key to a confraternity room above the sacristy to the firm of undertakers, Antonio Almeida and Company. He wanted to be free of civil and ecclesiastical responsibility.

Dr. Lisboa has recorded that Senhor Almeida himself spent the night of February 23 in the church, accompanying each group of pilgrims in a separate, orderly way to the room above to see the body. Dr. Lisboa wrote:

"He [Almeida] was deeply impressed by the respect and

devotion with which the people approached and kissed the little corpse on the face and on the hands, and he remembers very clearly the live pinkness of the cheeks and the beautiful aroma which the body exhaled. At last on February 24 at 11:00 a.m. the body was placed in a leaden coffin which was then sealed. Present at this act were Senhor Almeida, the authorities and several ladies . . . who declared that the body exhaled a beautiful aroma of flowers as the coffin was being sealed. Owing to the purulent nature of the disease and the length of time that the body remained unburied, this fact is remarkable. In the afternoon which was wet, the funeral took place on foot, in the company of a large crowd."

The cortege ended at the Rossio Station, and the train carried Jacinta's remains to the vault in Ourem. It was Shrove Tuesday. Tomorrow Lent, the season for penance and prayer would begin. For Jacinta, that season, lengthened to 33 months, had ended. She had kept it well. With a gaping wound in her side she left this life on her Good Friday. Mary came for her soul. And the tired and broken instrument of prayer and pain, her body, gave an aromatic forecast of a glorious resurrection.

In Lisbon, Dr. Lisboa excused his late arrival at a General Annual Conference of the St. Vincent de Paul Society. He explained that he had been on a work of mercy, the burial of one of the seers of Fatima. Many of the assembly, which included some of the most prominent Catholics of the capital, laughed at his expense. The Cardinal Patriarch joined them. Later he became a strong believer in Fatima, and had a great desire to celebrate Mass in the Cova before he died. But in 1920, except for a small number of priests and a very devoted and fairly large number of the laity close to the events, Fatima had not won acceptance. It is not easy to be a prophet.

Chapter Eight

The Real Story

The real story of Jacinta is the story of her growth to spiritual maturity. The three apparitions of the angel and the six of Our Lady were dramatic highlights of that growth. There is good evidence that God favored her with various other such vivid mystical experiences. They were frequent toward the end of her life, according to the testimony of Mother Godinho and others. Lucia takes for granted that Jacinta was on speaking terms with Our Lady. There are external proofs, such as her predicting that she would go to two hospitals and die alone. She also predicted correctly the deaths of two of her doctors and her two sisters, Teresa and Florinda.

In her last illness, she heard the fine sermon of a certain priest praised. His voice and delivery were admired. Jacinta said: "When you least expect it, you will see that padre is wicked." He left his priestly duties within a year in circumstances of scandal.

She had several mystical glimpses about a pope of the future (at least her future). Lucia recounts two in the third Memoir. "One day during siesta, we went to my parents' well. Jacinta sat on the stone slabs of the well while Francisco and I climbed up a bank nearby to look for honey in a thicket of brambles. A little while later Jacinta called to me, 'Didn't you see the Holy Father?' 'No.' 'I can't say how but I saw the Holy Father in a very large house, kneeling before a table with his face in his hands. He was crying. Many people were in front of the house; some were throwing stones, while others were cursing him and using foul language. Poor Holy Father. We need to pray a lot for him.' "

Another time the children were praying at the Cabezo. When they finished, Jacinta called Lucia: "Don't you see many, many roads, highways and fields jammed with people weeping with hunger for they have nothing to eat? And the Holy Father praying in a church before the Immaculate Heart of Mary? And many people praying with him?" Lucia had seen none of this.

But all of these experiences taken together are just highlights or more evident signs of the transformation of soul the Holy Spirit was making in Jacinta. She was a chosen child of grace. God's favors did what they always do. To whom ten talents are given, ten more will be demanded. The special graces left an invitation to a corresponding response in proportion. This response calls on the person's generosity. It means a greater emptying of all that is selfish. It means a more detached and glowing love for God's creatures. It means also much thinking and praying on the part of the mystic. That person has to fill in, to come to understand and correlate with the rest of experience from more ordinary sources, the new material God has freely provided. Perhaps it means more than anything, much suffering. This suffering comes in part from the groping darkness of the mind trying to fill in the gaps between these high spots. It may come from the misunderstanding of others, for a mystic such as Jacinta is set on a lonely course. It may come from the demands for deliberate penance inherent in the greater vision, or from the merciful bestowal of affliction and illness allowed by God from natural causes.

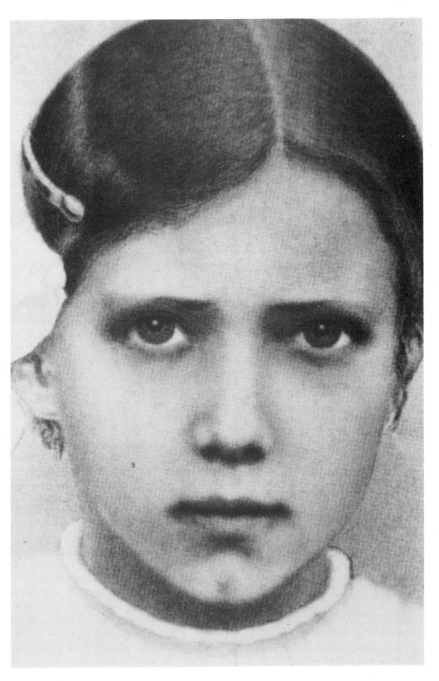

1. *Jacinta Marto (1910-1920)*

2. *Left to right: Jacinta, Francisco and Lucia.*
Photo taken on July 13, 1917, the date of the third apparition.

3. Left to right: Jacinta, Lucia and Francisco.
This photo was taken in the garden of Jacinta and Francisco's home.

4. *Left to right: Jacinta, Lucia and Francisco.*
A photo taken at the site of the apparitions in the Cova da Iria.

5. *Manuel (Ti) and Olympia Marto, parents of Jacinta and Francisco.*

6. A. *Top: The room where Francisco died.*
   B. *Bottom: Lucia's house.*

7. *Jacinta and Francisco's house. A photo taken in the 1950's. Their mother Olympia is standing in the doorway.*

8. *The parish church of Fatima, where the three seers were baptized.*

All of these parts of the response taken together—generosity, selflessness, detachment, thinking, praying, doing penance, suffering—add up to growth in spiritual maturity. It is the real story of Jacinta. It began with the quality of the soul God gave her, with the environment of faith in her early years. It heightened with the visits of the angel, and it came to full growth in the 33 months from Mary's first visit, May 13, 1917 to Jacinta's last breath, February 20, 1920. Jacinta came out a heroine. Archbishop Fulton Sheen calls her "one of God's little giants, who was wise beyond all learning." Fr. John DeMarchi says that already at the age of 7, "Jacinta was a kind of earthbound angel, whose virtues even when told with deliberate restraint, will sound to many like pious exaggerations."

Jacinta's generosity was complete from the beginning. She wanted to miss no opportunity to save souls from hell. She was a worrier about details. A picture that comes to mind that may help in understanding Jacinta is that of a bride getting ready for the wedding. She wants to make sure nobody is missed in the invitations. She is careful about choosing her dress, about the ceremony. Jacinta wasn't getting ready for a wedding, but was trying to get everybody ready for heaven. Her constant worry that people might go to hell was just the other side of that hope for their reaching heaven. It was as strong as a bride's might be whose parents were ill and might die before her wedding. It was a great burden for anyone to carry; for Jacinta in her generosity and her natural meticulousness and her child's view of the size of sins, this fear for others' going to hell entered into the deepest part of her own personality. Lucia says that from the July vision on, Jacinta was a changed person. "She even changed her disposition." This change came with Jacinta's response of complete generosity.

Jacinta always wanted to make sure that nothing was lost,

that no drop of good for somebody's soul leaked out from a faulty intention. It wasn't enough to be doing an act of self-denial. She had to make very sure that the act was properly directed and went as the straightest arrow to its target. Speaking of their making sacrifices, Lucia says, "Whenever we agreed to make one or when we had something to suffer, Jacinta used to ask, 'Did you already say to Jesus that this is for His love?' If my answer was 'No,' she would say, 'Then I will say it to Him,' and joining her hands she raised her eyes toward heaven, and said, 'Jesus, this is for your love and for the conversion of sinners.'"

Francisco especially wanted to console Jesus and Mary. This thought was foremost in his mind. He had been told from the beginning that he must say many rosaries. So the rosary became his constant companion. Francisco did not correct people. He just moved away, left the area, if there was cursing, lying, gossip, bad stories or language.

But Jacinta, natively bashful and at home only in very congenial company, spoke up. She corrected people. Lucia tells about it in Memoir IV:

"If in her presence children or even adults said something or performed any action less than proper, she would reproach them, saying, 'Don't do that. You are offending God, and He is already offended enough.' If the person or child answered back, calling her a fake pietist, or a little saint of worm-eaten wood or something similar, what happened several times was that she would look at them with a certain severity, and go off without saying a single word."

These rebuffs hurt Jacinta as they would anybody. They hurt her in a stronger way for the more unusual reason, always uppermost in her mind, that the person was again offending God, and making heaven less sure.

All three children found that they wanted to be more with one another. The depth of their experiences together made a bond between them that made them seek one another's company. Lucia, older, more out-going, was also more ready to succumb to the persuasions of her girl friends to go back to their dressing up and parties. Francisco reproved her on this occasion. He and Jacinta shied away more from some kinds of amusement and friends, if they felt any threat to their constant awareness of their mission in life of consoling the Hearts of Jesus and Mary and saving sinners.

The three children often talked about what sacrifices they had made and would make, and about all that Mary had said. They were ingenious in finding ways to make sacrifices which their parents and families would not know about. They counted up their sacrifices and encouraged one another.

It was with them, not a game, not a means of self-pursuit or vanity. The pursuit was for souls to be saved, for war to be averted, for bringing comfort to Jesus and Mary. "Do you know why Jesus is so sad, Lucia?" Jacinta asked in her last illness. "Because Our Lady has explained how much He is offended and still nobody cares; they just go on with the same old sins."

The touching thing about Jacinta is the completeness of her giving. Her cast of mind, her selflessness, her love for Jesus and Mary and each person pushed her on. Her giving can be measured only on the scale of the heroic. It demanded so much of her. She often lay still in bed, in the position she was placed. To toss and turn in bed with a fever or when in much pain, seeking momentary relief, is a near necessity. One day when Lucia and Jacinta were telling each other the sacrifices they had made, Jacinta said: "In the night I had pains and I offered Our Lord the sacrifice of not turning over in bed, and for that reason I didn't sleep at all." Sometimes while Francisco was still alive, she wanted to visit him, but delayed for awhile, making this a sacrifice to help a sinner.

At the same time, she had that quality of readiness to be guided which sets off the false visionary from the true. The pastor of Olival had a good way of putting things. "If you feel like eating some particular thing, let it go and in its place, eat something else, and offer the sacrifice to God." She could also appreciate and follow the inverse logic of making to God a sacrifice of not making a sacrifice, when occasion demanded that. So, with such willingness, a path was cut through varying circumstances that allowed for completeness in giving without destroying moderation.

Jacinta gave back to Lucia the piece of rope she wore. This was shortly after she got sick. Francisco had done the same. Jacinta told Lucia, "Keep it because I'm afraid my mother might see it. If I get better, I want it again." The piece of rope had three knots and was somewhat spotted with blood. Lucia kept it and Francisco's until she left home for the convent school at Oporto. Then she burnt both of them.

At the first meeting in May, Jacinta told Lucia to ask if the Lady were hungry. When she found out, especially in July, that the Lady's hunger was for souls, Jacinta, like a solicitous little hostess, never tired in trying to alleviate that spiritual hunger. In her last days when the Blessed Virgin appeared to her and told her she would no longer suffer, Jacinta related that Mary looked very sad and told her the cause of her sadness: "The sins which lead the greatest number of souls to perdition are the sins of the flesh. Luxurious living must be avoided, people must do penance and repent of their sins. Great penance is indispensable." Jacinta entered into her sorrow. "I feel so sorry for Our Lady. I feel so sad."

Jacinta was all heart. As most little girls her age might

hug a baby doll, Jacinta hugged and kissed a picture of the Sacred Heart. She later asked for and was brought a picture of the Immaculate Heart. Her affection was liberally bestowed on it. She knew the two Hearts belonged together. Because she was selfless and all heart, she felt the sorrows and wept for the needs of other people. Her first thought was always for sinners. The Holy Father came right after them. He had a constant champion, an affectionate little friend in Jacinta. Often she thought of his need for prayers. He always got three extra Hail Mary's after the rosary.

One time she had met a soldier who was crying because he had orders to go to war. His wife and three children had to be left behind and his wife was ill. Jacinta invited him to say the rosary with her, and assured him. "Don't cry, Our Lady is so good. I am sure she will get you the grace you are asking for." His orders were canceled the day before he was to leave. Jacinta never forgot him. He received one extra Hail Mary after the rosary from then on. We think of the poem, *The Trimmins on the Rosary*, in which the special intentions and special persons came on endlessly, getting special mention and the extra Hail Mary. Jacinta's life was a kind of perpetual *Trimmins on the Rosary*.

She and the ones she prayed for were close. Distance meant nothing to her. She bridged with her outgoing little heart the distance to Rome and the unseen Holy Father, the distance to the unknown priest who was suspended from his duties, and the distance to all the unknown sinners she was praying and sacrificing for. When she heard about the priest, she burst into tears. She said on that occasion that people should pray for and not talk about the priests. Jacinta was socially a kind of separatist. She was not outgoing in the usual sense of readiness to mix and share her feelings and thoughts. Thus, more than life's ordinary loneliness touched her. Hers was the lonely path of the great mystics.

Most of them reach their spiritual maturity as adults. They learn to adapt to social demands. Jacinta reached spiritual maturity in childhood. The necessary aloneness for that could find no compensations or adaptation at her age. She had to be lonely because her heart was so outgoing. There were few she could share it with of any age.

Lucia answered the question about how other people felt around Jacinta (Memoir IV). She said that it was a hard question to answer, but she could report on what she felt and on what she observed in the exterior acts of others.

"What I felt was what one feels ordinarily when one is around a holy person, who seems to be communicating with God in everything. Jacinta always had a serious, modest and affable character, which seemed to translate the presence of God in all her acts, common to people already advanced in age and of great virtue. I never saw in her that frivolity or enthusiasm typical of small children for ornaments or play. This was after the apparitions, because previously she was the leader in enthusiasm and caprice."

"If I was close to her, in no time there would be dozens of children around us, but if I went away she would be alone. Meanwhile when they were close to her, they seemed to enjoy her company. They would hug her with hugs suitable to innocent caring. They liked to sing and play with her . . . In her sickness, when I went to visit her, I used to find a fairly big group waiting for me to go in and see her. It seemed that a certain respect stopped them . . ."

When Lucia asked if Jacinta wanted some of the children to stay, she answered, "Fine, but just those smaller than I." The little ones were glad to stay. Jacinta sang with them, taught them prayers and, when able, sat on the floor and played games with them. But the children would not come back on their own. They would wait for Lucia to bring them in or even for Jacinta to call them. There was a kind of restraint.

Ladies of the village sometimes would come and bring their sewing. They liked to be near Jacinta. They felt a supernatural atmosphere around her. They felt the same around Francisco. "We just came from talking to Francisco and Jacinta. Close to them we feel a kind of supernatural atmosphere we do not know how to explain." They asked Lucia to explain it. She shrugged her shoulders and kept silent. "Very often I heard people comment on it," she said.

There are really no rules for a spiritual director to follow that will provide complete support and understanding for a child like Jacinta. She needed tutoring beyond their capability. Nor did she lack it. The Blessed Virgin continued to take personal care of tutoring her eager pupil in the painful process of dying to self, so that God's gifts may better live in self and others. Jacinta deserves to be called the littlest victim soul. Her special vocation was to keep making an offering of herself in the truest and least selfish form. Her consuming and ever-present interest was to give of herself. Mary led her through the emptying process this demands. Gradually Jacinta reaped on earth the rewards of detachment from all selfishness. She became more contemplative, more acutely aware of true values, more full of God's presence, more able to see into the hearts of others.

The wisdom of her last months shows a soul in close touch with God, filled with some of that knowledge another Child showed in the temple at Jerusalem.

Dr. Joaquin Alonso wrote and compiled a work of 18 volumes as the official documentation on Fatima. He goes into detail on all the sayings attributed to Jacinta in her final months. Some, he upholds, some he says are not authentic. One that is often quoted is this: "Fashions will much offend

Our Lord. People who serve God should not follow the fashions . . ." Dr. Alonso, when asked about this particular one on a U.S. tour in 1975, replied in the careful way of a scholar that he affirmed the authenticity of some texts attributed to Jacinta. "And these latter are sufficient to draw the conclusion that Jacinta received special light concerning the care which Christians must have concerning this important point of Christian moral education."

One of the sayings attributed to Jacinta that has more meaning today than it did in 1920 is this: "Doctors do not know how to cure people properly, because they have not the love of God." Today there is more room left in the art of healing for the influence of human love and the more hidden workings of spiritual well-being. When Jacinta was asked who taught her these little capsules of wisdom, she replied, "Our Lady, but some of them I thought myself. I so love to think."

This answer at once gives evidence of two things. It tells us that sayings attributed to Jacinta should not be prefaced by "Our Lady said," and it also tells us that Jacinta is a prophet in her own right. She assimilated her deep mystical experiences granted in the main visions, in others of a private nature, in the constant cooperation of her soul with daily grace. She combined these with the more ordinary learning received from instruction and the experiences of life. She achieved a harmony, a maturity far beyond her age. This is her real story. If the Church raises her to sainthood, this will be the real reason. She will be a saint because she was heroic in virtue, and generous and selfless in giving. She will be a saint because she put her whole heart into the Peace Plan offered by the Immaculate Heart of Mary.

The Peace Plan and You

All that has been set forth so far now comes to one focus. It raises one question. You are in the focus. The question is: What will you do for peace? Jacinta has been presented as a prophet for our times. She lived and died in the twentieth century. As a child prophet sent by God, she proclaims truth in the direct and unmistakable way of a child. There are no big words. There is nothing hard to understand about her core message.

Since her message has to do with peace, it is meant for anybody really interested in helping to bring peace to the world. That would mean all persons of good will. Her message is not just for Catholics, nor for all Christians. It is a call to everybody. Peace is of interest and value to people everywhere. With today's weapons for total destruction, when unimaginable horror could engulf the human race and wipe out nations and destroy our civilization, the call to do what you can to win peace is urgent and insistent.

None of the ancient prophets, warning the people to amend their lives, had more reason to tell of the heavenly voice speaking to them, than does the youngest prophet in our era. And more than any of the ancient people do we have reason to listen and to respond.

What we need is something beyond rhetoric. We need

something specific. We need something more than a bow to the idea of peace, or the expression of a good intention. Therefore for those who can accept Jacinta as an authentic prophet, with a God-given message showing the path to peace, specific and simple suggestions are given here. God does not necessarily call each person to exactly the same part in fulfilling His Peace Plan. Still, He does not want to eliminate any person of good will. Peace is for all. So the Peace Plan is for all.

The first suggestion embodies the core message. *Amend your life and pray*. Do this according to the *3H* way that comes out so strong in the life of Jacinta. Her way centered on the three "H's" of Heaven, Hell and Heart.

The first "H" in her life is *Heaven*. She had an assurance that she would go there. She also had the guarantee that it wouldn't be long; as time went on she even knew the exact time and hour. What this knowledge did for her was to telescope everything in, to bring it up to close vision. It made other things seem to be of lesser proportion. In fact, keeping heaven in mind brings everything else into truer proportion. You learn how to hope for truer, more lasting values. You learn how to bounce back better after some loss, even a lost love. For you haven't lost heaven, and you still have God's love. You have the hope of getting to heaven, meeting Jacinta and legions of persons who will give you more love than the sum of all possible love on earth. Popes and presidents, masters and servants, canonized saints and one-time sinners will all be there. Everything will be harmony and order. There will be perfect peace, for peace is the tranquility of order. There will be no lies, no dishonesty, no jealousy, no fear or hate, no mistreatment of any kind. The creature will be in just the right relationship to the Creator. A joyful song of praise and thanksgiving will fill every soul.

The second part of the *3H* way of Jacinta is *Hell*. Jacinta did not see the battlefields. She saw something far worse. She saw hell. Her unselfish love went out to everybody. She wanted to save everybody from hell that she possibly could. She knew wars are minor and temporary hells where the disorder of sin comes to a visible boil. She knew that they give only an idea of the major and lasting hell, where the disorder of sin comes to a presently invisible boil. Therefore she wanted to prevent sin. That is why she worried so much about people. That is why she gave so generously of her pain. She knew God would use it to save others from the pains of hell, and along with that from the punishments of war.

Her courage in trying to face hell and war—the whole of it—points the way for everybody. If you accept her as a God-given prophet, it also points a finger at you, reminding you to face hell and war and sin in a personal way. Take yourself out of danger from the first, and you will have taken, to a degree, others away from danger both of hell and of war. Think of hell in a realistic way. Don't be a cliff-hanger over hell. Amend your life.

To help in facing the reality of hell, a list may be jotted down of the names sins have been given: pride, covetousness, lust, envy, anger, jealousy, sloth, dishonesty, slander, lying, cheating, robbery, murder. If you visualize the trouble and pain and discord these may have brought into your own life, then add all this up. It gives a glimpse of hell. If you think of the pain that people bring on themselves and others by drinking, drugs, marital infidelity, neglect of family, and add these up, again you get an image of hell. If you think of the meaning of regret for missed opportunities, for work undone, for lack of courage, again you find by adding them all together an idea suggesting the regret of hell. If you think of people who have disliked you or hated you, or tried to ruin your good name (or think of yourself on the giving

end of such things), then add this up and place yourselves
together as a one-room family: you have some image of the
company in hell. There nobody is for anybody else. There is
no love, no sympathy. Everybody is against the other and
against the Creator.

The third "H" in her way is *Heart*. If you could understand it as Jacinta and her brother Francisco did, you would
also have a clearer picture of the first "H" which is for
heaven. They were allowed to see into the most perfect of all
merely human hearts. Mary did not have to show the
children a vision of heaven. She just showed them her
Heart. They then had such a glimpse of heaven and its joys
and love that they longed to go there. The Immaculate
Heart images heaven, for it shows the perfect order of
heaven, where all creatures have an ideal relationship to
each other and to the Creator. This Heart images heaven,
for it gives a picture of love at its best.

A good clue in understanding the Heart presented to the
children is the joy and ease it brought to them. After the
angel's visit, they were happy but could not talk about it.
When the Lady came, they communicated eagerly and easily. Her visit let them just be themselves.

The benefit to you in trying to capture Jacinta's spirit
here is that you will gradually come to know perfect acceptance. You can be perfectly yourself, at ease and happy in
trying to do good. Your accomplishment grows, but the
effort seems less. As St. Augustine says, where there is love,
there is no work, or if there is work, the work is loved. God's
commandments are presented to you, written on a perfect
Heart. They will not seem harsh nor burdensome when
thought of in this way. That Heart shows the infinite com-
passion of God who gives the commandments. It reminds
you that God, whose justice provides for an unending hell,

has a corresponding mercy that is best symbolized by the most tender and perfect Heart of a woman.

No matter what sins you have committed, how negligent or ungrateful you may have been, how long it is since you sincerely repented, the mercy of God still calls you. God doesn't speak as a voice booming from the heavens. Rather it is His will in these days to personify His mercy in an Immaculate Heart, and call you in the soft and charming voice of a woman. "Why don't they give up sin?" The voice of the youngest prophet echoes the pleading of the Heart that, of all mere creatures, loves God and all His creatures best.

Prayer is part of the Peace Plan. Prayer is necessary because it is a primary part of the right order of relationship of creature to Creator. The Immaculate Heart is a prayerful Heart. There is no amendment of life without prayer. Prayer draws on the reservoir of strength that God supplies to do one's duties with fidelity and perfection. Prayer for others shows the highest kind of love for them. It recommends your friend or relative to the highest source of goodness, and says: Be good to the one I love. Prayer for others shows that your heart is in the right place. The model presented in the Peace Plan is the most perfect of creature hearts, the Immaculate Heart of Mary.

In order to follow through on Jacinta's *3H* way, a simple, minimal prayer program is suggested. The wording can be altered to accord with the wishes or conscience of each person:

> "I offer God this day all I think or do or say."
>
> "Sweet Heart of Mary be my salvation."
>
> "I ask Jacinta to say for me, Sweet Heart . . ."
>
> "O God (*or* O my Jesus) forgive us our sins,
> save us from the fires of hell,

and lead all souls to heaven,
especially those who have most need of your mercy."
"O God (*or* O Most Holy Trinity) I believe in You.
I adore You, hope in You and love You.
I wish to make amends for those who do not believe,
adore, hope or love."

One prayer was most recommended in the Peace Plan. At each visit of Mary the children were asked to pray and get people to pray the rosary. When asked for her name, the Lady said she would give it at the last visit, thereby giving to her declaration the impact of suspense. The giving of the name also was timed to come in the month of October, traditionally set aside in the Catholic Church as the month of the rosary. Finally Mary answered the question. "I am the Lady of the Rosary." As in the earlier visits she held a rosary in her hand. Mary called on all who follow Christ to pray the rosary.

The second suggestion then, is for all Christians. The call of Mary is not limited to Catholics, any more than the celebration of Christmas or Easter is limited to them. The truths or mysteries celebrated in those two great feasts are two of fifteen called to mind in the rosary. Other great events called to mind in the rosary and celebrated by all Christians are the Ascension of Jesus into heaven and the coming of the Holy Spirit at Pentecost. So are all the events that go with Good Friday. The major events of the childhood of Jesus from conception till the age of 12 when found in the Temple are brought to mind in the rosary. All these are in the Bible and are treasured by all Christians.

These events and the truths connected with them are termed mysteries. The ones just mentioned make up thirteen of the fifteen rosary mysteries. They are events and truths that draw us into the mystery of ourselves and God.

By thinking of them we come to better answers about who we are, why we are here and what God wants of us. Thinking of them, going around this little circle of events and truths brings a person into contact with the most visible and clear showing of God's plans ever presented to the human race. They are called mysteries because they deal with sublime truths which link God and man. Take this little circle of mysteries and you have a solid center. Lay out the rest of your life and the life of all people around it in concentric circles, and you have the answers to the deepest problems of life: the meaning of joy and sorrow, of mercy and justice; and how to reach our final goal: happiness and glory in heaven.

The two final mysteries of the rosary bring that happiness to mind. They dwell on the reaching of that goal by the purest of creatures. Representing the hearts of all of us, first of all in love for the Creator is the Immaculate Heart of Mary. That Heart was not left to decay in a tomb, for Mary was assumed into heaven body and soul. There as first among angels and men she took her place as Queen. All the mysteries of the rosary culminate here. Her victory is ours. Of all the people who ever walked the paths of earth, of all the angels who honor the Creator and help us, there is none holier, none closer to the Supreme Being, none more unique of His mere creatures. In Mary we have the best image of what we long for. In her we have our hope personified. St. Bernard put it in a phrase which for almost a thousand years has raised the hearts of men: Hail Holy Queen, Mother of Mercy, our life, our sweetness and our hope!

The victory of Mary culminating in her Assumption and Crowning as Queen is also the great victory of Christ. She is the first of the redeemed, the greatest fruit of His sacrifice. There was a time when there was no Mary. She was nothing, non-existent. From this nothingness God the Father called her into being. God the Son redeemed her, and God the Holy Spirit made her His spouse, the best visible representative and cooperator in giving His gifts.

It is not hard to see why Our Lady recommended the rosary as the best peace prayer. The rosary is a handy formula, already made venerable by several centuries' use by millions of Christians. It has helped many people to keep the truths of the gospel in mind day by day. It has done so because it is simple and handy and visible. You don't have to be able to read to use the rosary. Through history this has been the lot of most people. Even today a great portion of mankind cannot read. But even for the greatest scholars, the rosary still is a handy formula for remembering the central truths of Christianity and going over them in a measured way.

The rosary is defined as a way of meditating on the joyful, sorrowful and glorious mysteries in the life of Christ and the Church, accompanied by the reciting of the Lord's Prayer and Hail Mary's. These vocal prayers provide the background, the measured beat. The Hail Mary itself is a compendium of Christianity for the individual. "Hail Mary, full of grace" recalls the moment of Jesus' conception. This is the beginning of hope for each person. "At the hour of our death" recalls the longed-for moment of glory, when all that Jesus did for each person will climax in meeting Him face to face.

Over our meditation, over the soft beat of the vocal prayers, the Dove hovers. The Holy Spirit who inspired the gospels delights in this simple summary. The Holy Spirit who inspired the 150 psalms delights in 150 Hail Mary's that are reminders of the psalms. The complete 15-decade rosary was the people's psalter in the Middle Ages. Those who could not read or could not join the monks in reciting the psalms, said Hail Mary's instead when the monastery bells rang out their invitation seven times a day.

In the course of time, the people's psalter, or Our Lady's Psalter came to be called a rosary, meaning a garland of roses. The beautiful notion of bringing roses to Mary, of crowning her with a garland of roses was added to the earlier practices. Custom gradually made the term, *rosary*, mean the five-decade one we ordinarily see and use. This is the one asked for at Fatima. The lady used the Portuguese word meaning one-third of the 15 decades. "Continue to say the Terco," she said.

The 15 mysteries are divided into three series: five joyful, five sorrowful and five glorious. Rev. J. Neville Ward, an English Methodist minister, wrote a book on the rosary and titled it *Five for Sorrow, Ten for Joy*. In this book he offers a series of meditations on the rosary, and recommends the use of the rosary by Christians in general. He says: "I am sure that one of the most hopeful means of realizing Christian unity is for Christians of one tradition to seek to share another tradition's experience of the riches of Christ."

The titles of the mysteries bring out in themselves the riches of Christ. The Joyful Mysteries consider these riches from conception till the age of 12. They are: 1) the Annunciation, when Jesus was conceived; 2) the Visitation when His mother visited Elizabeth and was greeted with the words, "Blessed are you among women and blessed is the fruit of your womb"; 3) the Birth of Jesus at Bethlehem; 4) the Presentation of Jesus in the temple; and 5) the Finding of Jesus after three days. The Sorrowful Mysteries cover the events of Good Friday: 1) His Agony in the Garden; 2) His Scourging; 3) the Crowning with thorns; 4) the Carrying of the Cross; and 5) His Crucifixion and Death. The Glorious Mysteries are: 1) the Resurrection; 2) the Ascension of Jesus into heaven; 3) the Coming of the Holy Spirit; 4) the Assumption of Mary into heaven; and 5) the grand Coronation of Mary as Queen.

The rosary leads to the Immaculate Heart of Mary. Her Heart and Joseph's were shaped by the mysteries they lived through, and which the rosary leads us through in their company. As Mary's Heart is a perfect copy of all God's laws, so does the rosary help to stamp these laws more on our hearts. St. Paul wrote to the Corinthians that they were a letter of Christ, written not with ink, but with the Spirit of the living God, not on tables of stone, but on the fleshy tables of the heart. The rosary will help to write the message of Christ on our hearts. In our daily rounds, in our contact with many people, some will read the message. Some will be helped to follow it better. All this helps to prepare the world for peace.

And God who carefully balances justice and mercy will be pleased. In the hidden ways of providence, the delicate balance swinging the world to nuclear destruction or to a new era of peace will adjust itself to the right side, and mercy will prevail. "He shall judge among the nations, and shall rebuke many people. They shall beat their swords into ploughshares, and their spears into pruning hooks; nation shall not lift up sword against nation, neither shall they learn war any more" (Is 2:4).

The life of Jacinta illustrates how God in His goodness allows us to share in the work of His providence. She is completely behind the scenes. There is no visible connection between her and most of the people she wants to help. God, through the ministry of Mary or through angels, perhaps, makes the connections. The little girl's sacrifices help some sinner unknown to her, to turn aside from his sin, to repent. He acts as usual with freedom, but a help has been given to enlighten his mind and strengthen his will. He uses his freedom to choose God's way. What Jacinta has done is to make reparation, to help swing the balance to the side of mercy. Language limps in trying to explain this. But it comes down to the basic principle that where some do not do their part, God allows others to make up, to offer compensation. The sacrifice of Jesus is complete and infinite. But God in His generosity and goodness, wants many to share in bringing the fruits of Jesus' sacrifice to individuals. It is part of the overall plan we see in operation day by day whereby God provides for our material needs. God the Creator has made everything. He has more than provided for our wants. Yet many must cooperate in bringing the good things He provides to one another. So, God the Son has redeemed all. He has more than provided for spiritual needs. But He needs, according to His plan, the participation of many. One helps bring the fruits of redemption to the other. Since some are shirkers or sinners, others may take a double or triple load. Jacinta offered to take all the load that the Hearts of Jesus and Mary sent her. She offered herself in short as a victim soul.

This idea of compensation or making reparation is at the heart of what the Blessed Virgin asked for at Fatima. It is the intimate secret of winning God's mercy. Therefore it is the intimate secret of winning peace. If the multiplied sins of millions deserve punishment for the world, then the sacrifices and prayers of others behind the scenes will deserve to bring peace.

The special work asked of Catholics is the making of the Five First Saturdays in reparation for sins committed against the Immaculate Heart of Mary. Lucia, in a letter of June 12, 1930 to Fr. Joseph Bernard Gonzalves, S.J., her spiritual director, described the way the First Saturdays are made. "For five months, every First Saturday, receive Holy Communion, say the rosary, pay a 15 minute visit to Our Lady while meditating on the mysteries of the Holy Rosary, and go to confession with the same goal in mind. This can be done on another day, as long as one is in the state of grace when one receives Holy Communion."

Lucia then mentions the great promise attached to making the Five First Saturdays. "Those souls who in this manner try to make reparation to me [this is Our Lady speaking] I promise to assist [them] in the hour of their death with all the necessary graces for their salvation." Bishop John Venancio calls this the greatest promise ever made in an authentic apparition. In the same letter to Fr. Gonzalves, Lucia writes: "The practice of this devotion will be equally accepted on the Sunday following the First Saturday, when for just motives, many priests will allow it."

Cardinal Leo Suenens of Belgium wrote about God's plans for Mary and our gratitude when we come to understand them:

"True Marian devotion commences from above, not below; and it is commanded by faith not emotion; it is above all, adherence to God and acceptance of His plan for her. It is an integral part of our right intention toward God. For Christian rectitude begins by voluntary adherence to the plan which God has willed, by rallying to God who traces, as it pleases Him, the trajectory of His grace. God has willed to associate Mary with His work of salvation. Through her He gave His Son to the world. Now the gifts of God are without repentance, and this 'order' no longer changes. The mediation of Mary remains forever, in accord with the plan of God . . .

"We do not have the right to prescribe the limits of divine action or to bypass intermediaries which He has freely chosen. It is God's right to love us with abundance and superabundance and to communicate to His creatures the glory to be His instruments. In God there is a place for all excess and it is only at our level that one economizes. Our filial devotion toward Mary is nothing but gratitude for the excess of divine love of which she is the living and permanent proof. It would be a grave error to consider Marian piety as a useless surplus obstructing our religion toward God.

"This piety is not a kind of refinement, a concession to the imagination and to popular sensibility, a cheaper way of salvation. It is for all without distinction the expression of God's saving will for us . . ."

For Catholics the invitation to win the peace may be responded to by having a new confrontation with Mary and with the Blessed Sacrament. This can have a definite, immediate start by making the Five First Saturdays. For all Christians, the invitation to win the peace may be accepted by praying the rosary. For everybody of good will without exception, the invitation to win the peace may be acknowledged by following Jacinta's *3H* way.

Jacinta left the legacy of a life, short and intense. Some people may shake their heads with a certain sadness over it. It seems a loss to them of the joys of normal childhood. God does not want this for children, they may say. God does not want this in such intensity from all children. He called Jacinta to a very special, very serious kind of life. He did this for the saving of souls and the creating of conditions to bring peace through His mercy. He did this for our example.

The words of Leon Bloy may be helpful:

"No one seems to realize that sanctity is a supernatural gift which differentiates one man from another just as if their very natures were changed. Nor does this come about suddenly or little by little. It is something which occurs in the profundity of God, in the silent depths of His will. The saint, like a genius, is a man apart, as lonely, as solitary, as alone of his kind as would be a plant that might have strayed down to us from the Garden of Eden. There is no road leading from talent to genius; so vast is the distance between the highest peak of virtue and the lowest valley of sanctity that all the torrents of the universe could flow unhindered in the vast, intervening space."

Whether you want to subscribe entirely to this picture or not, it does make clear that the saint has a special calling. Whether or not he or she is canonized, the person chosen by God to deliver a message has to do so in a unique and special way.

Jacinta wrote for us in large print. She printed out in her life the words of the message of the Lady much as a child would in laboriously printing out the words on a sheet of paper. But you can read them. They are so clear and so much to the point that the message comes through better than would several pages written by an adult.

The average person, unlike Jacinta who printed the message of the Peace Plan in big handwriting, will write it out in a smaller script. Prayer and sacrifice will be distributed over more years. But if you put all the prayer and sacrifice in one summary, it will also come out strong and large, as a love story. It will show a heart moulded on the Sacred and Immaculate Hearts, big enough to love many not till death, but beyond death. To love a person beyond death means to be concerned about what happens to them beyond death. One who loves this way will find it easy to say: "Lead all souls to heaven, especially those who have most need of Your mercy." For 33 months, this is the way Jacinta Marto said to everybody: "I love you."

Jacinta looked at evil point blank while holding on to the comforting and reassuring hand of Mary. She represents for everybody the *3H* way. Not everybody, it is true, looks at evil in her way. They try to find various escapes. But she shows the way. Everybody can understand it. Look point blank at heaven and hell, and hold on to the hand of a

Mother who reassures you that God is merciful and wants you in heaven. The youngest prophet shows the utterly simple way, which is yet the spiritually mature way.

Jacinta prayed the rosary and got others to pray it. She never made the Five First Saturdays. What she did most of all was to feel the pain of others, and the greater their need, the more she felt their pain and offered her prayers and sacrifices for them. She never forgot the soldier whom she had seen crying. She always added an extra Hail Mary to her rosary for him. He was no relative, no special friend. She had just felt his pain and seen his tears. She felt the pain of the Holy Father. He always received 3 Hail Mary's after the rosary. But when she made her intentions, sinners came first. The Holy Father was added usually right after the sinners. *Her preoccupation with hell flowed from this same feeling for other people's pain.* Her endless questions about what kind of sins people committed to deserve hell, her hope for Mary to show hell to everybody, her exactitude in offering things with just the right intention, all came from a basic feeling for others' pain, and a consuming hope for their happiness.

Jacinta then is the one whom the greatest number of people can follow. If she is canonized, many people may feel more like putting her on their knee rather than on a pedestal. She calls the young, the meek, the shy, the unsuccessful, the ones who can't read or write. She has something in common with them. She calls anyone who can feel the pain of any other person; she calls the generous and the thankful.

Jacinta also calls those who have a long drawn-out sickness or any deep, lasting problem or affliction. They all can convert their pain into helping people get to heaven and avoid the pain of hell. Theirs is a very special calling, that of joining Jesus in His redemptive sufferings.

Above all she calls those whom she tried to help most during her short life here, especially those who have most need of God's mercy. You can picture Jacinta in heaven, peering over the edge, trying to catch the attention of someone about to fall into hell. She calls for them, and she calls as Mary first called her. "Don't forget," she says, "many souls are lost because there is no one to pray and make sacrifices for them." In short she calls for you, because she wants to help someone avoid the pain of separation from God for eternity. She calls for your separation from some luxury or minor necessity, and primarily for the sacrifice of reforming your life, where it is in need of closer conformity to God's will.

At the beginning of her first Memoir, Lucia wrote a lovely prayer-poem about Jacinta. It is a fitting note on which to end our consideration of the youngest prophet.

> You on the earth lived flying,
> Lovely Jacinta,
> In much suffering Jesus loving.
> Remember the plea I send to you,
> Be good to me.
> Before the throne of the Virgin Mary
> Lily of candor, shining pearl,
> There in heaven you live triumphant.
> Seraphim of love,
> With your little brother at Our Lord's feet,
> Pray for me.

Appendix A

QUESTIONING by Fr. Manuel Nunes Formigao (1917)

Fr. Formigao was appointed by the administrator of the partriarchate of Lisbon from the beginning of the rumors about the apparitions to investigate the situation. He was present at the September and October apparitions. His first interview with the children was on September 27, 1917. He also interviewed them on the day of the great miracle, October 13, and then returned on the 19th to clear up a discrepancy about when the still raging World War would end, to interview them again. Before the October vision, he had also had a preliminary interview on October 11th.

Fr. Formigao signed his books and articles with a nom-de-plume, *Viscount de Montelo*. His September interview was in Lucia's house, as was the one on October 11th. On the 13th of October the interview was at Jacinta and Francisco's home, and also the one on the 19th. On October 13th he had also walked with Jacinta to her home and asked some questions. Fr. Formigao returned for still another interview on November 2, 1917.

In the interview of October 13 he asked Jacinta:

"Besides the Virgin, whom did you see today at the Cova da Iria?"

"I saw St. Joseph and the Child Jesus."

"Where did you see them?"

"I saw them near the sun."

"Did you also see near the sun, Our Lord, the Mother of Sorrows and the Virgin of Carmel?"

"No."

"But you told me on the 11th that they would appear."

"Yes, Lucia saw the other Virgin, but I did not see her."

"Was the Child Jesus on the right or the left of St. Joseph?"

"On the right."

"Standing, or in St. Joseph's arms?"

"Standing."

"Did you see the right arm of St. Joseph?"

"No."

"How tall was the Child Jesus?"

"He didn't reach St. Joseph's waist."

Jacinta and Francisco definitely did not see the final three apparitions which Lucia saw near the sun. They saw St. Joseph, and Jesus standing as a little child of one or two years of age to his right.

Lucia saw Jesus being held by St. Joseph. She saw the final three apparitions: Our Lord, Our Lady of Sorrows and of Mt. Carmel. Even Our Lady of Mt. Carmel was a bit hazy in definition. It seems that these last visions were meant for Lucia alone and indicated her vocations to the Sisters of St. Dorothy and the Carmelites.

INTERVIEW with Fr. Thomas McGlynn, O.P. (1947)

Fr. Thomas McGlynn, O.P. in one of his interviews with Lucia in February, 1947 asked her about the rosary.

"I would like you to state the importance of the rosary in the message of Our Lady."

"My impression is that the rosary is of greatest value not

only according to the words of Our Lady at Fatima but according to the effects of the rosary one sees throughout history. My impression is that Our Lady wanted to give ordinary people who might not know how to pray this simple method of getting closer to God."

"Did Our Lady ask for the Family Rosary?"

"Not expressly."

"Does Our Lady request that every Catholic recite the rosary every day?"

Lucia dealt first with the restriction of the rosary to Catholics. "She didn't express in particular, but everyone in general."

The word Mary used for the rosary was *Terco*. This is a common Portuguese term for the five-decade rosary. But on October 13th, Mary gave her name saying, "I am the Lady of the Rosary." The word used at that time was *Rosario*.

Fr. McGlynn at this same interview then asked about devotion to Our Lady of Mt. Carmel.

"Was devotion to Our Lady of Mt. Carmel recommended?"

"In the fourth apparition at Valinhos she said that Our Lady of Mt. Carmel, Our Lady of Sorrows, St. Joseph and the Infant Jesus would come to bless the world."

"Did Our Lady say anything about the scapular?"

"No."

"Was devotion to Our Lady of Sorrows recommended?"

"No."

Fr. McGlynn asked for an account of the series of apparitions in October. Lucia replied that Our Lady appeared at first as usual, then at a certain point, turned her hand toward the sun. People then heard Lucia say, "Look at the sun." She does not remember exclaiming in this way. Lucia saw near the sun at this time the series of apparitions. "Then appeared at her side, first St. Joseph and the Child Jesus;

then Our Lord, then there were changes of light in which Our Lady took on different aspects—Our Lady of Sorrows and Our Lady of Mt. Carmel. While this was going on the people cried out that they saw the phenomenon in the sun. I myself did not see it." Lucia was also not aware of other things people saw, colors in the sky and showers of flowers. She also offered this information: "When the Bishop made his first visit to Fatima he saw a shower like rose petals; then he believed."

Fr. McGlynn asked about Jacinta.

"Jacinta is reported to have said of those who die in war that nearly all of them would be lost. Did Our Lady say this?"

"I don't remember her [Jacinta] saying this. Our Lady never said anything about those dying in war going to hell." Lucia offered an explanation about the mistaken quote. "I don't know whether it was through revelation or intuition, but Jacinta had visions of people dead in the streets from war. Jacinta in horror said: 'Can it be that most of these will go to hell?' This was her own [Jacinta's] reflection."

"Did Our Lady say a certain Amelia would be in purgatory until the end of the world?"

"True."

"How old was Amelia?"

"Eighteen."

When Fr. McGlynn said this troubled people, Lucia replied that she did not think it very remarkable, since one could go to hell for all eternity for missing Mass on Sunday.

The interviews above, made in 1917 and 1947, are given as samples of careful investigation. They too are subject to evaluative scrutiny. But they teach us that we must be careful and exact in our own way of speaking. Often everything is summed up under the broad expression: *Our Lady of Fatima said*. In all reports of mystical experience, it is ultimately the visionary who speaks to us. The visionary's authentic experience must be exactly put, and carefully separated from later experiences and personal comment and opinion.

At Fatima, the three visionaries had individual mystical experiences and later, individual favors of grace. This indicates that it is still more necessary to avoid the lump summing up of everything with the expression: *Our Lady of Fatima said*. For instance, St. Joseph has a definite connection with the Peace Plan. But it was not Our Lady of Fatima who said: "The sound of victory will be heard when the faithful recognize the holiness of St. Joseph." That is a prediction of Isidore of Isolanis, a 16th century Dominican theologian.

Appendix B

More on the Fatima Secrets

(For a description of the July Fatima vision, see pp. 27-39.)
In the minds of the children, the heart of the second part of the *secret* was not in the prophecy of contingent future events. It was in the devotion to the Immaculate Heart. There was to be a direct relationship between the spread of such devotion and to these events either happening or not happening. In short, God wants devotion to the Immaculate Heart of His Mother. If enough people respond, many souls will be saved from hell, there will be peace, and a great war will be prevented.

In the light of what happened, we can deduce that enough people did not respond, and so World War II happened. Had enough responded, the course of history would have changed. The "unknown light" mentioned as a sign, was widely noted at the time. It was seen the night of January 25-26, 1938. Astronomers called this phenomenon an Aurora Borealis. But Lucia in the third Memoir tends to differ with them. "I can't say for certain, but it seems to me that if they inquired further they would see that it was not and could not be, in the form in which it appeared, such an Aurora."

As promised in 1917, the Blessed Virgin came back to Lucia, along with the Child Jesus in 1925, when she was a postulant of the Dorothean Sisters in Pontevedra, Spain, to ask for the First Saturday Devotion of Reparation to the Immaculate Heart. The Child Jesus repeated the request two months later. In 1929, in a major mystical experience at Tuy, Spain, Our Lady told Lucia that the time had come to ask for the consecration of Russia to her Immaculate Heart. Lucia communicated these requests to her confessors. She also wrote to the Bishop of Leiria and the Holy Father a number of times, especially as the approaching rumbling of World War II grew louder. Her request to the Holy Father was for the consecration of Russia to the Immaculate Heart. She hoped for a last-minute reprieve from the catastrophe of World War II, and the spread of communism. The Portuguese bishops did consecrate Portugal to the Immaculate Heart, and Lucia in her letter of December 2, 1940 to the Pope, said that she expected Portugal to be spared from the war. History attests that despite much pressure from Germany and the U.S., Portugal remained neutral.

Pius XII consecrated the Church and the world to the Immaculate Heart with a descriptive mention of Russia on October 31, 1942. On July 7, 1952 he wrote a letter consecrating Russia to the Immaculate Heart in a more specific way. Pope Paul VI reaffirmed the consecration at the Second Vatican Council in 1964, and on his 1967 pilgrimage to Fatima on the golden anniversary of the major apparitions. He said that he came as a pilgrim for peace in the world and for unity in the Church.

Some writers have objected to Lucia's later reports of visions, and have said that we can't accept her as a pipeline to heaven. No, we can't. That is true. But Mary in 1917, as was stated then by the children, wanted Lucia to live on. Jacinta and Francisco, as was also stated then, were to die soon. Implicit in the external, observable lives of the children, then, is the conclusion that Lucia still had some special work to do. She is not a pipeline, but she is a mystic. In view of the rest of the Fatima story, what she says can well be received with respect, and subjected to the usual criteria of judgments applied to those God sends to us as prophets.

The third part of the Fatima *secret* has never been made public. It has been a subject of much controversy, questioning and acrimony. On February 11, 1967, Cardinal Ottaviani made a public statement about the *secret* as the golden jubilee was being celebrated in Rome.

"Lucia has written in Portuguese, on a sheet of paper, what the Holy Virgin asked her to say to the Holy Father. The envelope containing the *secret* of Fatima was handed to the Bishop of Leiria, and though Lucia has told him he might read it, he wouldn't do that. He wanted to respect the secret, perhaps as a sign of respect to the Holy Father . . . Always closed, it was given to Pope John XXIII. The Pope opened the envelope and read its contents. Though the text is written in Portuguese, he told me that he had understood it thoroughly. Then he himself put it into another envelope, sealed it and laid it in one of those archives which are like a deep and black, black well in the bottom of which no one sees anything at all . . . The secret is a matter for the Holy Father to whom it was addressed. It was he who was the addressee. And if the addressee of the secret has decided not to declare: 'Now is the moment to make it known to the world,' we must be content with his wisdom which wished it to remain a secret . . ."

We may recall the words of Ti Marto when Jacinta first used the term "secret." "A secret is a secret, and so it should be kept." Fatima is not about possible catastrophes primarily. The real message and secret of Fatima concerns the will of God about the Immaculate Heart of Mary and how doing His will or not doing it in this matter can spell out a future of war or an era of peace. God has entrusted peace to the

Immaculate Heart of Mary. If we understand this, we hold an important key to the future of the world. The importance of Jacinta is that she is a little, chosen prophet of God, to tell us about and demonstrate to us parts one and two of the Fatima *secret*. Part one is about hell. Part two is about the Immaculate Heart. If part three of the Fatima *secret* deals with a contingent future war and catastrophe, the contingency may hinge on how well and how many people follow the youngest of the prophets.

Appendix C

St. Joseph's Role in the Peace Plan

(For an account of the apparition of St. Joseph, see pp. 49-62.)

A case history can be made to illustrate the importance of St. Joseph from the families of the Fatima children. Lucia had a harder time of it because her good mother dominated the scene, constantly trying to force her to say she was lying. Her father, also a good man but not strong enough, evaded the issue by allowing Maria Rosa to have her way, and by saying, "These are women's tales." In Memoir IV Lucia says that her uncle said immediately on hearing that the children and he were summoned to Ourem: "They cannot walk that distance, and not being used to horseback riding, they cannot keep themselves on the ass. Furthermore, I have no reason to present two children this age in a courtroom." The verdict in Lucia's case was: "Let her answer. I don't understand anything about these things, and if she is lying, it is well that she is punished." Lucia fell off the donkey three times on the 18-mile round trip to Ourem and back.

The Cova belonged to her family. But with the influx of crowds, they weren't able to plant anything. Garden and grass were trampled down. Lucia's mother cried; her sisters said, "You should eat only what is grown in the Cova da Iria." Her mother often struck her. If we analyze the situation, we come back to lack of leadership on Antonio's part. Maria Rosa was a very good and devout mother who loved her child. She often tried to make up later for fear she might make Lucia sick, and because she did love her. She was also ill. No doubt she would have been a difficult person to get along with under any circumstances. Antonio simply was not strong enough. He did not take a father's rightful place as head of the family.

Lucia, in an interview with Martin and April Armstrong in 1953 said: "He was a good father. He worked from morning to night and gave every penny that we needed to his family . . . He worked his own property, but he worked for others too . . . He was not a drunkard . . . My father died most suddenly, but his things were well in order . . ." She says that like many other men, he stopped in the tavern after Mass on Sunday to talk to friends and have a drink. But all in all he was a hard-working, responsible and loving father. He was, in short, what a great many men are; but he could not cope with the blows of life. Manuel (Ti) Marto to a much greater degree reflected the character and strength of St. Joseph.

Martin and April Armstrong describe him as they met him in 1953. (Had Jacinta lived to that date she would have been 43). "A small, grizzled, grinning man came to the wooden gate. He wears a long black stocking cap, the *carapuca*, which serves all the mountain men as head covering and carry-all for tobacco and lunch. He wears an incredibly patched suit. Once a brown pin-stripe, it is mended all over in blue and black and grey serge. A costume designer would reject the outfit as exaggerated, but nothing could more perfectly convey the unself-conscious poverty and the comfortable dignity of his life." He was 82 at the time, still working daily. His wife, Olympia was 84.

Ti Marto was not a very good advance man for St.

Joseph, at least not in the one summary statement he made to the Armstrongs. They asked, "Next to Our Lady who is your favorite saint?" He answered: "I have none. I pray to God, to Our Lady and to Jesus Christ. The others are all the same thing, you know. My favorite prayer is the Our Father. It's *Our* Father, not my Father. So, when I pray it, I pray it for all." Ti Marto's life in words and deeds does illustrate the expected ideals and principles of a man modeled on Joseph.

He had a great reliance on divine providence, a characteristic of Joseph. All through the Fatima events, as each crisis came up, he had a solution reflecting his trust in God. He made no attempt to find out any secret. His trust in God allowed him to trust in his children, and respect their dealings with God. He was not over-protective. He could have laid down strict orders for the children not to go to the Cova, to guard them from possible injury. Had he been a self-centered father, the Administrator could not have gone off with the children because they would have been fearful of getting into the carriage. They felt free of pressure. They were able to make up their own minds, though here they made a mistake. The self-centered, domineering father allows no room for mistakes. He did not shield Francisco and Jacinta from questioning. His house was over-run with inquiring visitors, even to their walking on the beds. His attitude of liberty was also extended to others. "When the house is full," he said to the distraught Olympia, "nobody else can get in."

Ti Marto's reliance on providence and his forgiveness came out in the drama of August 13. He helped to quiet the angry mob. The father of two kidnapped children had every right to be angry. A weaker man would have broken down, given vent to some momentary feeling of self-pity, or expected sympathy. Bloodshed would have been a blot on the Fatima appearances. No doubt the devil worked hard to thwart Mary's Peace Plan in its infancy. Ti Marto showed the Joseph quality of reliance on providence and instant forgiveness that made him a man of peace, and helped Our Lady continue her work.

August 13 and 15 are a miniature of what goes on among nations. Francisco and Jacinta's father shows the path to peace: moderation, reliance on providence, forgiveness of injuries, being a brother's keeper, doing good to those who injure you. To sit down and have a drink with the man who kidnapped your children, in order to protect him from violence is the mark of a man after the heart of Joseph. It demonstrates Christ's words: "Love your enemies. Do good to those who persecute you" (Lk 6:27). To the question: "Which way will we find peace?" he answered, "If the people say the rosary, peace will be. If they don't hear the word of Our Lady, there will be another war. Peace is easy. We need only to unite against evil. What more could we need to do?"

The Joseph-quality he showed that is easiest to understand was his continuing, loving relationship with his wife Olympia. In the background of this, too, stands the dependence of both on providence. "My Olympia and I have been married 55 years. And we are still sweethearts. We are a big joke around here, the way we carry on. Sometimes someone will say to me: 'Here, Ti Marto, here is a sweet.' And I say: 'Good, I will give it to my girl friend.' She still calls me her boy friend. Aha. One of these days, I always say, we will get married and settle down. But now we are still courting. . . ."

In this love of the parents for each other, we come to understand the soul of Jacinta. In jail she mentioned her mother when crying that she would never see her family again. But her parents were not divided. Their love came to her to support a very sensitive nature. Like the Little Flower of Jesus, Jacinta had a father who was both strong and gentle, whose love for her mother brought her security and peace. She could continue to grow in love for God and man. She could accept God as a loving Father, even though His justice demanded a hell. The office of St. Joseph in relation to the human development of Jesus was the same. Joseph's trust in providence, his allowing liberty for growth (even though Jesus used it to stray away for three days), his constant love for Mary—all these provided for the Child Jesus the model He also needed to know, humanly speaking, of the justice and mercy of God the Father.

Joseph is the man of peace, keeping all the laws of his church and his government, yet fleeing to a strange country to save the life of the Child. He is a model of respect for authority, but did not let unjust authority take over. He is a model of moderation with justice. He shows this in his painful decision to put Mary away quietly in the face of her inexplicable pregnancy. Joseph was strong and gentle. Though least in dignity in the Holy Family, he acted as husband and father, and provided the strength and support that comes from the unity of having a head.

The father must take his place, not as a tyrant, but as a man of love. Like Joseph who found the measure of his love in the deserving heart of Mary, husbands need wives who have a deserving heart like Mary's. The love of Mary and Joseph for each other provides the model. When men start to measure themselves by St. Joseph, the day of peace will come to nations. When all start to measure their hearts by the Immaculate Heart, God's Peace Plan will be fulfilled.

Appendix D

The Golden Rose

At 11:00 a.m., May 13, 1967 the papal legate, Cardinal Cento presented the Golden Rose to the Bishop of Fatima, Joao Venancio. The ceremony took place in front of the Fatima Shrine Church as 800,000 pilgrims watched. On the Golden Rose assembly were written the words: "Paul VI, imploring the protection of the Mother of God upon the Church, dedicated the Golden Rose to the Sanctuary of Fatima, May 13, 1967."

The Golden Rose is a papal sign of special honor and recognition. It is blessed on Laetare Sunday in Lent, sometimes known as Rose Sunday. The custom goes back at least to the time of Pope Leo IX who referred to it in 1050 as an ancient custom. The Golden Rose has been given to churches, countries and cities, and also to rulers and other individuals who have shown some special love for the Faith.

When the Golden Rose was given at Fatima, Bishop Venancio saw in it a way of calling attention to the consecration of the world to the Immaculate Heart, and of confiding the entire human race to the Mother of Heaven.

To the surprise of the bishops of Portugal and everyone, Pope Paul VI himself addressed the gathering immediately after the address of his Legate, Cardinal Cento. He said in part:

> In this moment we too desire to be in union with you, dear children, to lift our prayers to the Mother of God and Our Mother that she may turn her maternal gaze upon the world still so far removed from her Divine Son, and to obtain a sincere and full reconciliation of all men to God.

Pope Paul's letter accompanying the Golden Rose made clear its meaning in connection with the Peace Plan of Fatima.

> In the last full session of the Ecumenical Council which had just approved the *Constitution on the Church* in the same moment when we proclaimed her Mother of the Church, in the same way that our predecessor, Pius XII of recent memory in hours of extreme world anguish consecrated the world to the Immaculate Heart of Mary, . . . so we too, considering the very grave injustices which now afflict us, confide (the human race) to the care of the Virgin Mother herself.

The Golden Rose of May, 1967 may well symbolize the dramatic action of Pope Paul VI on November 21, 1964 when he announced that he would send the Golden Rose to Fatima, and at the same time proclaimed Mary Mother of the Church. The action was dramatic for it was at the closing session of the Second Vatican Council in 1964 in St. Peter's, before the assembled bishops of the world. After a moment of stunned silence, the bishops stood, removed their mitres and applauded. Some shed tears of joy. It would be hard to find a setting more complete to accent approval of the Peace Plan of Fatima.

Appendix E

Pope John Paul II Thanks Our Lady of Fatima

On May 13, 1982 Pope John Paul II went to Fatima to thank the Blessed Mother for preserving his life the year before. He went to the spot where the visions took place in 1917, now covered by the Capelinha, a small chapel that looks something like a picnic-grove shelter. He prayed in silence while the great crowd of at least a million people waited. Later he told them that he came as a pilgrim among pilgrims to give thanks. In his first audience after his recovery, he recalled that he had been shot at the hour and on the day of the original 13th of May appearance of Mary. John Paul II also spoke with Sr. Lucia and had his picture taken with her. He went to the tombs of Francisco and Jacinta in the church and prayed at each, first at Francisco's and then across the front part of the church to the tomb of Jacinta.

In precise language he recalled that Pius XII had consecrated the world to the Immaculate Heart, and said he came here to do the same.

> Today, John Paul II, successor of Peter, continuer of the work of Pius, John and Paul, and particular heir of the Second Vatican Council, presents himself before the Mother of the Son of God in her Shrine at Fatima.

In what way does he come? He presents himself, reading again with trepidation the motherly call to penance, to conversion . . . The successor of Peter presents himself here also as a witness to the immensity of human suffering . . . Peter's successor presents himself here with greater faith in the redemption of the world . . . My heart is oppressed when I see the sin of the world and the whole range of menaces gathering like a dark cloud over mankind, but it also rejoices with hope as I once more do what has been done by my predecessors: namely I entrust the world to the Heart of the Mother. I entrust especially to that Heart those people which need particularly to be entrusted.

Appendix F

*Pope John Paul's Letter to the Bishops Asking for Acts
of Entrusting the World to the Blessed Virgin*

In a letter dated December 8, 1983, feast of the Immaculate Conception, Pope John Paul II wrote to the bishops of the world asking for Acts of Entrustment of the world to the Immaculate Heart of Mary. He suggested that a fitting date would be the Feast of the Annunciation, 1984, anticipated (because of the Third Sunday of Lent) to March 24, or on March 25, the Sunday. With the letter he included an Act of Entrusting.

The letter and the Act follow. (*Origins* vol. 13, no. 38, pp. 627-629)

Letter to the Bishops

On March 25, 1983, we began the extraordinary Jubilee of the Redemption. I thank you once again for uniting yourselves with me in the inauguration, on that same day, of the Year of the Redemption in your dioceses. The Solemnity of the Annunciation, which in the course of the liturgical year recalls the beginning of the work of the redemption in the history of humanity, seemed to be a particularly appropriate time for that inauguration.

This beginning is linked with Advent, and the whole of the present Year of the Redemption has in a certain sense the character of an advent, in that the year 2000 since the birth of Christ is drawing near. We live this time of waiting for the fulfillment of the second millennium of the Christian era, sharing the difficult and painful experiences of the peoples, indeed of all humanity in the contemporary world.

From these experiences is born a particular need, in a certain sense an interior imperative, to direct ourselves with renewed intensity of faith precisely to the redemption of Christ, to its inexhaustible salvific power. "In Christ God was reconciling the world to himself . . . and entrusting to us the message of reconciliation" (2 Cor 5:19). The Synod of Bishops, which took place last October, drew our attention in the same direction.

On this present day, the Solemnity of the Immaculate Conception, the Church meditates on the salvific power of the redemption of Christ in the conception of the woman destined to be the mother of the Redeemer. In this there is a further stimulus in order that, in the context of the jubilee, in the face of the threats to contemporary humanity, which have their roots in sin, there be made a more intense appeal to the power of the redemption. If the way to overcoming sin passes through conversion, then the beginning of this way and likewise its successive stage can only be in the profession of the infinite salvific power of the redemption.

My dear brothers!

In the context of the Holy Year of the Redemption, I desire to profess this power together with you and with the whole Church. I desire to profess it through the Immaculate Heart of the Mother of God, who in a most particular degree experienced this salvific power. The words of the act of consecration and entrusting which I enclose, correspond, with a few small changes, to those which I pronounced at

Fatima on May 13, 1982. I am profoundly convinced that the repetition of this act in the course of the Jubilee Year of the Redemption corresponds to the expectations of many human hearts, which wish to renew to the Virgin Mary the testimony of their devotion and to entrust to her their sorrows at the many different ills of the present time, their fears of the menaces that brood over the future, their preoccupations for peace and justice in the individual nations and in the whole world.

The most fitting date for this common witness seems to be the Solemnity of the Annunciation of the Lord during Lent 1984. I would be grateful if on that day (March 24, on which the Marian solemnity is liturgically anticipated, or March 25, the third Sunday of Lent) you would renew this act together with me, choosing the way which each of you considers most appropriate.

Act of Entrusting

1. "We have recourse to your protection, holy Mother of God."

As we utter the words of this antiphon with which the Church of Christ has prayed for centuries, we find ourselves today before you, Mother, in the jubilee year of the redemption.

We find ourselves united with all the pastors of the Church in a particular bond whereby we constitute a body and a college, just as by Christ's wish the apostles constituted a body and college with Peter.

In the bond of this union, we utter the words of the present act, in which we wish to include, once more, the Church's hopes and anxieties for the modern world.

Forty years ago and again 10 years later, your servant

Pope Pius XII, having before his eyes the painful experiences of the human family, entrusted and consecrated to your immaculate heart the whole world, especially the peoples for which by reason of their situation you have particular love and solicitude.

This world of individuals and nations we too have before our eyes today: the world of the second millennium that is drawing to a close, the modern world, our world!

The Church, mindful of the Lord's words, "Go . . . and make disciples of all nations . . . and lo, I am with you always, to the close of the age" (Mt 28:19-20), has, at the Second Vatican Council, given fresh life to her awareness of her mission in this world.

And therefore, O Mother of individuals and peoples, you who know all their sufferings and their hopes, you who have a mother's awareness of all the struggles between good and evil, between light and darkness, which afflict the modern world, accept the cry which we, moved by the Holy Spirit, address directly to your heart. Embrace, with the love of the mother and handmaid of the Lord, this human world of ours, which we entrust and consecrate to you, for we are full of concern for the earthly and eternal destiny of individuals and peoples.

In a special way we entrust and consecrate to you those individuals and nations which particularly need to be thus entrusted and consecrated.

"We have recourse to your protection, holy Mother of God": Despise not our petitions in our necessities.

2. Behold, as we stand before you, mother of Christ, before your immaculate heart, we desire, together with the whole Church, to unite ourselves with the consecration, which, for love of us, your son made of himself to the Father: "For their sake," he said, "I consecrate myself that

they also may be consecrated in the truth" (Jn 17:19). We wish to unite ourselves with our Redeemer in this his consecration for the world and for the human race, which, in his divine heart, has the power to obtain pardon and to secure reparation.

The power of this consecration lasts for all time and embraces all individuals, peoples and nations. It overcomes every evil that the spirit of darkness is able to awaken, and has in fact awakened in our times, in the heart of man and his history.

How deeply we feel the need for the consecration of humanity and the world—our modern world—in union with Christ himself! For the redeeming work of Christ must be shared in by the world through the Church.

The present year of the redemption shows this: the special jubilee of the whole Church.

Above all creatures, may you be blessed, you, the handmaid of the Lord, who in the fullest way obeyed the divine call!

Hail to you, who are wholly united to the redeeming consecration of your son!

Mother of the Church! Enlighten the people of God along the paths of faith, hope and love! Help us to live in the truth of the consecration of Christ for the entire human family of the modern world.

In entrusting to you, O Mother, the world, all individuals and peoples, we also entrust to you this very consecration of the world, placing it in your motherly heart.

Immaculate Heart! Help us to conquer the menace of evil, which so easily takes root in the hearts of the people of today, and whose immeasurable effects already weigh down upon our modern world and seem to block the paths toward the future!

From famine and war, deliver us.

From nuclear war, from incalculable self-destruction, from every kind of war, deliver us.

From sins against the life of man from its very beginning, deliver us.

From hatred and from the demeaning of the dignity of the children of God, deliver us.

From every kind of injustice in the life of society, both national and international, deliver us.

From readiness to trample on the commandments of God, deliver us.

From attempts to stifle in human hearts the very truth of God, deliver us.

From the loss of awareness of good and evil, deliver us.

From sins against the Holy Spirit, deliver us, deliver us.

Accept, O Mother of Christ, this cry laden with the sufferings of all individual human beings, laden with the sufferings of whole societies.

Help us with the power of the Holy Spirit to conquer all sin: individual sin and the "sin of the world," sin in all its manifestations.

Let there be revealed, once more, in the history of the world the infinite saving power of the redemption: the power of merciful love! May it put a stop to evil! May it transform consciences! May your immaculate heart reveal for all the light of hope!

Acts of Entrustment in the United States

The Holy Father's official representative in the United States, Most Rev. Pio Laghi, led the most representative of the Acts of Entrustment for the United States. On March 25, 1984 he celebrated the Mass, gave the homily and led the

Act of Entrusting in the National Shrine of the Immaculate Conception, Washington, D.C. The homily is printed in *Image*, a magazine devoted to Our Lady of Guadalupe as Patroness of the Americas (Box 29055, Wash. D.C. 20017).

There is a need to continue such Acts of Entrustment on all levels, national, diocesan, parochial and individual, and in religious communities cooperating as a group. This will insure the fullness called for to give the fullness of peace in the world.

Fr. John A. Ryan, S.J. (100 E. 20th St., Baltimore, MD 21218) and his Reparation Society would be a good source for inquiry about details of various Acts of Entrusting in the United States, and the debated question of whether or not Mary's Fatima requests regarding collegial consecration have been fully satisfied.

Appendix G

Beatification and Third Part of the Secret

On May 13, 2000 Pope John Paul II journeyed to Fatima to beatify Jacinta and her brother, Francisco. The ceremony had been originally set for April 9 in Rome, but at the urgent request of the bishops of Portugal, the Holy Father changed the date and place. The two children were to be the youngest ever beatified who were not martyrs.

A Plenary Assembly of the Congregation for the Causes of Saints had decided, April 2, 1981 that it was possible for such young children to have practiced virtue to a heroic degree and so fulfill the conditions needed for acceptance of their Causes. The Holy Father approved the decision and bestowed the title of Venerable on the children. The miracle required for beatification, the cure of a Portuguese woman, Maria Emilia Santos, paralyzed for 22 years, had been approved, June 28, 1999.

At the conclusion of the Mass of Beatification, May 13, Cardinal Angelo Sodano, Papal Secretary of State, made a surprising announcement. The Holy Father, he said, wished to make known the third part of the Secret of Fatima. It concerned a vision of the three children in which a Bishop in white was attacked and fell, apparently dead. The Holy Father believed that he himself was that Bishop. The Cardinal gave some details and comment but said that Sr. Lucia's actual letter describing the vision and a fuller explanation by the Sacred Congregation for Doctrine would be made later.

The beatification of Jacinta and Francisco, which would have been small news in big daily newspapers, served as the springboard to announce the third part of the Fatima *secret*. And so it shared in the headlines. Providentially, the occasion served to recount the entire Fatima message, including the heroic example of the children's lives.

On June 26, 2000 the full text of Sr. Lucia's letter about the third part of the secret was released, together with dates and details of its writing, manner of delivery and follow-up. A statement of Cardinal Joseph Ratzinger, Prefect of the Congregation for Doctrine, on divine and human revelation and a careful analysis of Lucia's letter concluded the booklet-size document.

Lucia's letter told of a vision of the three children in which they saw an angel with a flaming sword, and a Bishop in white who along with many others was making his way slowly and painfully toward a cross on a mountain. The ground was strewn with many corpses and the scene portrayed desolation and destruction. Finally the Bishop fell in a hail of bullets and arrows.

The Holy Father believes that the assassination attempt of May 13, 1981 in St. Peter's Square is the explanation for the Bishop who fell. He noted that the day and month were the same as those of the 1917 appearance of the Blessed Virgin to the children.

On the same date in 1982 he returned to Fatima to give thanks to Our Lady for "guiding the bullet" and saving his life. In fact, on the occasion of a visit to Rome by the Bishop of Fatima, he gave him the bullet, which had remained in the pope's car at the time of the assassination attempt. By the Bishop's decision the bullet was later set in the crown of the Blessed Virgin's statue.

The third part of the secret, as had been noted some years earlier, adds nothing essential to the core message of Mary. That message is a message of mercy, calling on us to do penance, especially that penance which is necessary to reform our lives, to pray, especially the rosary, and finally, to make the Five First Saturdays of reparation for sins that especially offend the Immaculate Heart of Mary. In this way the Immaculate Heart becomes our model for love and service of Jesus and more souls can be saved and the world can win a period of peace.

The document of June 26 also stated that the conditions specified by the Blessed Virgin for the consecration of the world and of Russia in particular to the Immaculate Heart had been fulfilled as the Blessed Virgin requested. So, there is no need to ask further about it. Sr. Lucia confirmed that the conditions had been fulfilled by the consecration made March 25, 1984 by the Holy Father. He had previously asked all the bishops of the Catholic world to join him in this Act of Entrustment. (Many believe that this Act had a large part in bringing about the collapse of the Russian communist empire in 1989.)

Of course, there is always room as time goes on, and in fact there is a continuing need for consecration by individuals, dioceses and countries. There is a continuing need in the face of threats to peace, to reform our lives, to pray the rosary, to make the Five First Saturdays. This is Our Lady's Fatima Peace Plan.

Sister Lucia's Letter

I write in obedience to you, my God, who command me to do so through his Excellency the Bishop of Leiria and through your Most Holy Mother and mine. After the two parts which I have already explained, at the left of Our Lady and a little above, we saw an Angel with a flaming sword in his left hand; flashing, it gave out flames that looked as though they would set the world on fire; but they died out in contact with the splendour that Our Lady radiated towards him from her right hand: pointing to the earth with his right hand,

*the Angel cried out in a loud voice: 'Penance, Penance, Penance!' And
we saw an immense light that is God 'something similar to how people
appear in a mirror when they pass in front of it' a Bishop dressed in
White 'we had the impression that it was the Holy Father.' Other Bishops, Priests, men and women Religious going up a steep mountain,
at the top of which there was a big Cross of rough-hewn trunks as of a
cork-tree with the bark; before reaching there the Holy Father passed
through a big city half in ruins and half trembling with halting step,
afflicted with pain and sorrow, he prayed for the souls of the corpses
he met on his way; having reached the top of the mountain, on his
knees at the foot of the big Cross he was killed by a group of soldiers
who fired bullets and arrows at him and in the same way there died
one after another the other Bishops, Priests, men and women Religious,
and various lay people of different ranks and positions. Beneath the
two arms of the Cross there were two Angels each with a crystal
aspersorium in his hand, in which they gathered up the blood of the
Martyrs and with it sprinkled the souls that were making their way to
God.*

Tuy-3-1-44 (punctuation as in the original.
The document gave a photo copy of
Lucia's own hand-written Portuguese)

On May 13 Cardinal Sodano had commented on this
letter. "That text contains a prophetic vision similar to those
found in Sacred Scripture, which do not describe photo-
graphically the details of future events, but synthesize and
compress against a single background, facts which extend
through time in an unspecified succession and duration. As a
result, the text must be interpreted in a symbolic key. The vision of Fatima concerns above all the war waged by atheistic
systems against the Church and Christians, and it describes
the immense suffering endured by the witnesses of the faith
in the last century of the second millennium. It is an intermi-
nable Way of the Cross led by the Popes of the twentieth century."

Cardinal Ratzinger in his extended comment and explanation on June 26 summed things up in a handy way: "'To save souls' has emerged as the key word of the first and second parts of the *secret*, and the key word of this third part is the threefold cry: 'Penance, Penance, Penance!' The beginning of the Gospel comes to mind (Mk 1:15) 'Repent and believe the Good News.' To understand the signs of the times means to accept the urgency of penance — of conversion — of faith. This is the correct response to this moment of history, characterized by the grave perils outlined in the images that follow. Allow me to add here a personal recollection: in a conversation with me Sister Lucia said that it appeared ever more clearly to her that the purpose of all the apparitions was to help people to grow more and more in faith, hope and love — everything else was intended to lead to this."

Referring to the painful progress of the Bishop in white and others amid a scene of destruction and death toward the Cross, Cardinal Ratzinger commented: "The Church's path is thus described as a Via Crucis, as a journey through a time of violence, destruction and persecution. The history of an entire century can be seen represented in this image. Just as the places of the earth are synthetically described in the two images of the mountain and the city, and are directed toward the Cross, so too time is presented in a compressed way. In the vision we can recognize the last century as a century of martyrs, a century of suffering and persecution for the Church, a century of World Wars and the many local wars which filled the last fifty years and have inflicted unprecedented forms of cruelty."

Cardinal Ratzinger also agreed with Cardinal Sodano that... "the events to which the third part of the *secret* of Fatima refers now seem part of the past."

Concerning the last part of the children's vision where the two angels gather the drops of blood shed by the martyrs and sprinkle them on souls making their way to God, Cardinal Ratzinger sounds a message of hope. He says, "The vision of the third part of the *secret*, so distressing at first, concludes with an image of hope: no suffering is in vain, and it is a suffering Church, a Church of martyrs which becomes a sign-post for man in his search for God.... There is something more: from the suffering of the witnesses there comes a purifying and renewing power, because their suffering is the actualization of the suffering of Christ Himself and a communication in the here and now of its saving effect."

He concludes with a mention of the famous expression "my Immaculate Heart will triumph." He goes on to explain: "the Heart open to God, purified by contemplation of God, is stronger than guns and weapons of every kind. The *fiat* of Mary, the word of her Heart has changed the history of the world because it brought the Savior into the world — because of her *Yes*, God could become man in our world and remain so for all time...."

Divine revelation is complete. It is summed up in Christ. But private revelations are not to be ignored. Cardinal Ratzinger quotes the *Catechism of the Catholic Church* (no. 67) "It is not their role to complete Christ's definitive revelation, but to help live more fully by it in a certain period of history."

The Fatima revelations ask us to join our hearts to the Immaculate Heart, to try to make them more like her Heart ever joined in love to the Heart of her Son. As more do this, more souls will be helped to salvation. When enough do this, then the Immaculate Heart will triumph and there will be peace in our world.

Jubilee Year, October 7-8

That the Holy Father wants continued living of the Fatima message was made evident later in the Jubilee Year. The climax of the Jubilee Year for him and the Bishops of the

Church had a definite Fatima accent. Before the Mass in St. Peter's Square, October 8, the statue of Our Lady of Fatima was carried in procession, preceded by the servers, deacons and Cardinals. The Holy Father walked behind it. The statue had been brought from Fatima at the pope's request. More than 1400 Bishops from around the world joined him for the rosary on October 7, and the Mass and Act of Entrustment, October 8.

The Holy Father explained: *"For our support and comfort, we have wished to emphasize during these Jubilee days the presence in our midst of Mary Most Holy, our Mother. We did so yesterday evening by reciting the rosary as a community; we do so today with an Act of Entrustment, which we will make at the end of Mass. It is an act that we will make in a collegial spirit, while sensing the closeness of the many Bishops, who in their respective Sees, are joining in our celebration and making this same Act together with their people. May the venerable image of Our Lady of Fatima, which we have the joy of hosting in our midst, help us to relive the experience of the first Apostolic College, gathered in prayer in the Upper Room with Mary, the Mother of Jesus."*

Before the final blessing of the Mass, the Holy Father led the concelebrating Cardinals and Bishops in making an Act of Entrustment to the Blessed Mother: *"...Today we wish to entrust to you the future that awaits us, and we ask you to be with us on our way.... We can turn this world into a garden or reduce it to a pile of rubble.... Today as never before in the past, humanity stands at a crossroads. And once again, O Virgin Most Holy, salvation lies fully and uniquely in Jesus, your Son.... We entrust to you all people, beginning with the weakest: the babies yet unborn, and those born into poverty, hunger and disease. We entrust to you all troubled families, the elderly with no one to help them, and all who are alone and without hope.... To you, Dawn of Salvation, we commit our journey through the new millennium, so that with you as guide all people may know Christ, the light of the world and its only Savior who reigns with the Father and the Holy Spirit for ever and ever. Amen."*

The pope then led the Angelus and gave the blessing. The statue of Our Lady of Fatima was carried in procession through the Square back into St. Peter's. The faithful sang the Salve Regina and the Ave of Fatima and waved handkerchiefs. This solemn and collegial honoring of Our Lady of Fatima with the Bishops of the Church proclaims with force the relevance of Fatima today. The story of Fatima, its message of peace, its practices of the Five First Saturdays, and its program of fidelity to duty, penance and prayer, especially the rosary has continuing meaning for our times and our future. There will be peace when enough people join in trying to make their hearts more like the Immaculate Heart of Mary.

(For the full Act of Entrustment see the *Bulletin of the Little Shepherds*, April-June, 2001)

Bibliography

Memorias e Cartas Da Irma Lucia (Composicao e impressai de Simao Guimaraes Filhos, LDA. Depositaria: L.E., Rua Nossa Senhora de Fatima, 296 - 5 Porto; Porto, 1973).
This work is the best and most basic available in English. The pages are arranged in three columns side by side, written in Portuguese, French and English. Occupying the left half of the opened book is a reproduction of Lucia's handwriting of the original. The editing, introduction and English translation are by Dr. Antonio Maria Martins, S.J., lecturer in Philosophy of the Pontifical Faculty of New Friburg.
The *Memoirs of Lucia* occupy 397 pages. The rest of the 467 pages (which are in finer print than the *Memoirs*) contain some of her letters and a few other documents written by her. The four Memoirs came out in 1935, 1937 and 1941. The third and fourth came out in 1941. This large book may be purchased at the Blue Army International Center in Fatima.

Fatima in Lucia's Own Words (Ravengate Press, Box 103, Cambridge, MA 02238 cloth $8.95, paper $4.95; Hard cover, 1976 199 pp.) Phone: (617) 456-8181.
This is the *Memoirs* of Lucia.
The *Memoirs* are also published by AMI Press (The Blue Army), Washington, NJ 07882 under the title of *Lucia Speaks*, 256 pp., paper.

The definitive work on Fatima has been printed in Portugal by Rev. Dr. Joaquin Maria Alonso who wrote and compiled the 18-volume work. He is the official Documentarian of Fatima, Editor of *Ephemerides Mariologicae* of Madrid, and a recognized Mariologist.

A Heart For All (AMI Press, Washington, NJ 07882 $6.50). This is the best book in English on the message and theology of the Fatima message. The work of six specialists, it came out of a meeting at the Blue Army Center in Portugal, August 16-22, 1971. The specialists are Canon Galamba de Oliveira, Dr. Joaquin Maria Alonso, C.M.F., Fr. Andre Richard, Archpriest John Mowatt, Fr. (now Cardinal) Luigi M. Ciappi, O.P., and John Haffert. Canon Oliveira took part in most of the canonical processes at Fatima; Fr. Alonso is the Fatima Documentarian; Fr. Mowatt resided at Fatima and cared for the Byzantine Chapel at the Blue Army Center; Fr. Ciappi was the Pope's theologian; and John Haffert is the foremost active promoter of the Fatima message among laymen.

The Immaculate Heart of Mary and *The Crusade of Fatima* are two books written by Fr. John De Marchi, I.M.C. who lived at Fatima from 1943 to 1950. He had many conversations with the parents of Jacinta and Francisco, with Lucia's sisters Maria dos Anjos, Gloria and Carolina, and with Maria de Capelinha and her son, John, custodians of the Chapel in the Cova. He also consulted with Lucia, who read and approved his Portuguese manuscript. *The Immaculate Heart of Mary* (Farrar, Straus, and Young, 1952) has a foreword written by Richard Cardinal Cushing. In it he says that the Fatima story is for all, not only Catholics; he says that all will find the book fresh and interesting and historical. *The Crusade of Fatima* was published early in 1947 (Reprint, 1964, Consolata Missions, Fatima, Portugal) and is a translation of Fr. De Marchi's Portuguese original, *Era Una Senhora*

Mais Brilliante Que O Sol, by Rev. Asdrubal Castello Branco and Rev. Phillip C.M. Kelly, C.S.C. Fr. De Marchi uses the writings of Fr. Manuel Formigao, who was present during the time of the apparitions, even on the day of the miracle of the sun.

Our Lady of Fatima William Thomas Walsh, (NY, Macmillan Co., 1947).

Mr. Walsh had a three hour interview with Lucia, July 15, 1946. He spent some time at Fatima, had conversations with the parents of Francisco and Jacinta, with Fr. John De Marchi, and others. His book has a good literary quality, and reads like a novel. It gives and captures the Fatima message well. In the light of a later sifting of facts, some details and impressions may not be accurate.

Fatima, Pilgrimage to Peace April Oursler Armstrong and Martin F. Armstrong, Jr. (Garden City, NY, Hanover House, 1954).

Mr. and Mrs. Armstrong describe their trip to Fatima, which includes interviews with Ti and Olympia Marto, the parents of Jacinta, and with Lucia. (Mrs. Armstrong assisted her father, Fulton Oursler for many years, and compiled his book *The Greatest Faith Ever Known* [Hanover House, 1954]). This book on Fatima has great readability, tying in personal impressions with the Fatima story and its relevance today. The message of Fatima in relation to Russia and communism comes through vividly.

Jacinta, the Flower of Fatima Fr. Humberto S. Medeiros & Fr. William F. Hill (Catholic Book Publishing Co., N.Y. 1946).

This work is an English translation and arrangement of Rev. Joseph Galamba de Oliveira's Portuguese original, and has a preface by (then) Msgr. Fulton J. Sheen. It has been reprinted and is now available through the Blue Army (Washington, NJ 07882). Fr. Medeiros, better known as the recently deceased Cardinal-Archbishop of Boston, gives many interesting details about Jacinta that do not appear in works about Fatima in which the whole Fatima story and not Jacinta in particular is the object. I believe it is the only book in English devoted to Jacinta besides the present one. After relating the events of the visions, there are 24 short topical chapters.

A Modern Crusader Fr. Eamond L. Klimeck, O.P. (London, Blackfriars, 1956).

As the title suggests, Fr. Klimeck is an enthusiastic crusader. The book includes an 11 page chapter on Jacinta, much of which is based on his interview with a blood relative whom he thought looked much like her. This book is the account of Fatima as it figured in the life and work of Fr. Klimeck and others associated with him.

Our Lady of Light Canon C. Berthas & Fr. G. da Fonseca, S.J. (Milwaukee, Bruce Publ. Co., 1947).

This is one of the Science & Culture Series of books of which Joseph Husslein, S.J. was General Editor. The Portuguese Jesuit, Gonzaga da Fonseca, professor at the Biblical Institute in Rome wrote a basic work, which was translated into French by Canon Berthas. This English language book is a translation and abridgment from the French. The first few chapters outline the Fatima story. The middle chapters are topical, and the last chapters provide documentation on various cures, physical and moral, and the interrogations of Fr. Formigao. A helpful gathering of prayers and the text of the consecration by the Portuguese bishops and Pius XII are included at the end of the book. The book is very well done and contains good photographs.

Fatima In The Light of History Costa Broshado, Transl. & Edited by George C.A. Boehrer (Milwaukee, Bruce Publ. Co., 1955).

The title tells that this book deals primarily with Portugal and its history, and how the Fatima events fit in with that history. The thesis is that Our Lady saved the faith in Portugal, which was then on the brink of losing it, beset by very strong and menacing enemies. The book has special value because it gives the reader a realistic background of the political and civic framework in which the Fatima events took place. The unsuspecting little children encountered evil forces which showed themselves in the many attempts to discredit Fatima. These same forces were working for the destruction of the Church itself and continued to do so. Portugal was spared the Communist revolution of Spain probably by the regenerative vitality of the faith, stemming from Fatima. The pictures taken at the Cova on October 13, 1917 are by Judah Ruah who came with the *O Seculo* reporter, Avelino de Almeida.

Vision of Fatima Thomas McGlynn, O.P. (Boston, Little, Brown & Co., 1948).

Fr. McGlynn's book is a collection of personal feelings built around his own experiences while making a statue of Our Lady of Fatima. He emphasizes the personal part taken in the creation of the statue by Lucia. He made the model from Feb. 8-14, 1947 at the Colegio do Coracao Sagrado de Jesus do Sardao. It is in a town across the river from Oporto, called Vila Nova de Gaia. Lucia was stationed here when she was a Sister of St. Dorothy. She spent much time there with Fr. McGlynn giving directions and demonstrating how Our Lady had held her hands at Fatima. Fr. McGlynn went to Rome before returning to the U.S., and Pius XII blessed his statue. Lucia made the rosary to hang on the right hand. (One of the decades has just nine beads!) Fr. McGlynn's book is very readable. It is also a work of art in its choice of comments and its humor. Like a statue, it is very precise in telling about the Fatima events. The recounting of the Fatima visions is a model of completeness and brevity without missing essentials. On the last page the author says that in April, 1948 Lucia entered the Carmelite Order at Coimbra.

Meet the Witnesses John M. Haffert (Washington, NJ, AMI, 1966).

Russia Will Be Converted John M. Haffert (Washington, NJ, AMI, 1956).

These are the two chief books of John Haffert concerning Fatima. As editor of *Soul* magazine and international lay head of the Blue Army, Haffert has written many works on Fatima in a constant stream for three decades. The titles of these books tell of their particular way of dealing with Fatima and its meaning. Both volumes have many interesting photos. Both have been checked by other Fatima experts for accuracy. Together they make up a panoramic view of the happenings at Fatima, of the development of devotion, the continuation of the Fatima story and of the expectations for the future, when peace will be restored to the world and Russia will be converted.

In *Meet the Witnesses*, Haffert gives the data gathered from the people at the great October, 1917 miracle of the sun. Fr. Galamba Oliveira, writer and expert on Fatima, says that this book is most interesting, a true enrichment of the bibliography on Fatima, and a challenge to today's incredulity.

Fatima, Portugal Und Sein Marienheiligtum Paul Dahm (B. Kuehlen Verlag, M. Gladbach, 1955).

This oversized book contains photographs of the 1917 era, and more recent times, not available in any English book. They convey a visual record that is well worth looking at, even if the reader cannot understand the German text. The six chapters are entitled: "A Look at Portugal," "The Land Around Fatima," "May 13, 1917," "The Place of Holiness," "A Day of Pilgrimage," and "For the Whole World."

Our Lady of Fatima Most Rev. Finbar Ryan, O.P. (Dublin, Browne & Nolan Ltd., 1948).

Ryan's book tells the Fatima story in direct, simple terms, interspersed with the Archbishop's personal reflections and his correlation of Fatima with doctrine and with important events in the Church of the Fatima era. Some details not mentioned in other English language books are also related, such as specifics about the March 6, 1922 bomb explosion in the Cova chapel. The bomb was one of five placed there.

Fatima, the Facts John De Marchi (Cork, Ireland, Mercier Press, 1950).

This work, written at the end of Fr. De Marchi's Fatima years, is authoritative, the fruit of a careful and lengthy sifting of his long study of Fatima.

Resources

Soul Magazine (Washington, NJ 07882). ($2.00 per year). *Soul* is the English language magazine of the Blue Army. It is published six times a year, and its only purpose is to promote the message of Fatima. The magazine is essential for anyone hoping to work fully for the same message.

Mother of Christ Crusade, Inc., 1444 Janie Ave., Billings, MT 59101 publishes Fr. De Marchi's work on Fatima in small-size paperback form. It is to be distributed free, not to be sold. Requests are generously fulfilled for a supply. Donations and a Dime-A-Day Club sustain this apostolate. It distributed 730,000 books in its first six months. The program began at the end of 1981.

Fatima Findings is a small monthly magazine, published since 1946 by the *Reparation Society of Mary Immaculate* 100 E. 20th St., Baltimore, MD 21218. Fr. John A. Ryan, S.J. is the editor. $4.00 a year and $4.50 foreign. Phone: (301) 685-7403.

Fr. Ryan reported in a phone conversation, April, 1985 that his daily Rosary Program has run steadily five days a week since it began on April 18, 1949. It is aired on Radio Station WDMD 750 AM five days a week, according to a sundown changing time schedule. Fr. Ryan thinks it may be the longest continuing radio program in the United States. It is supported by freewill contributions.

Fatima International P.O. Box 382, Temple Hills, MD 20748 publishes a magazine, and distributes the works of Robert Bergin of Australia. Mr. Bergin has devoted his life to spreading the message of Fatima. Phone: (301) 423-2358.

Our Blessed Lady of Victory Mission, Inc., R.R. 2, Box 25, Brookings, SD 57006. Phone: (605) 693-3983.
Fr. R. Tangen distributes Lucia's *Memoirs*, and allied Fatima material.

Fatima Or Moscow by Clementine Lenta (Marian Fathers Press, Stockbridge, MA 01262).
This 37-page pamphlet is practical, forceful and direct. P. 26 states that Cardinal Ottaviani read the letter of Lucia with the 1960 secret when Pope John XXIII finished reading it and passed it to him. Pope John sealed it and had it put into the Vatican Archives.
C. Lenta's works (Nina Publ., 23 East Buffalo St., Duluth, MN 55811. Phone: (218) 728-2049) always list handy addresses, and this one is no exception. It has a number of references for obtaining Fatima materials for further study.

VHS Tapes Eight hours on eight apparitions of Mary, distributed by M. Murtagh, Box 98 (St. George) Staten Island, NY 10301. Phone: (718) 816-5094.

Jacinta, Bright Star of Fatima sound cassettes 2 hours (Pope, P.O. Box 6161, San Rafael, CA 94903).

Golden One Productions, Inc. (P.O. Box 11054, Glendale, CA 92106)
is an apostolate asking people to keep the Fatima Peace Plan, and to pray in particular for the making of a large-scale TV production on Fatima, one that would have network saturation viewing over several evenings.

St. Gabriel Media, Inc. (P.O. Box 255, Farmington, MI 48024) produced an hour combo documentary-dramatic movie on Fatima. It is available to rent or buy on 16mm film or on video cassette - VHS. The cassette is sold for $49.00 plus

$5.00 shipping. The National Shrine, Washington, DC has a cassette for viewing on request at the Shrine.

Catholic Books on Tape (Ignatius Press, P.O. Box 18990, San Francisco, CA 94118).
The Children of Fatima by M.F. Windeatt is on 5 one-hour cassettes.

The Blue Army (Washington, NJ 07882) has in preparation a major feature-length movie on Fatima (1985), *The Great Sign.*

Mary Productions (58 Lenison Ave., Belford, NJ 07718)
Mary-Eunice, actress and script writer has video and sound cassettes on the major visions of the Blessed Virgin, including Fatima.

Natalie Martha Loya (23 Lockwood Ave., Yonkers, NY 10701. Phone: (914) 968-3576)
has a personal apostolate of giving lectures on Fatima, The Blue Army and other subjects.

The North American Voice of Fatima (Barnabite Fathers, Our Lady of Fatima Shrine, Youngstown, NY 14174).
This newspaper-style publication has a series entitled *Fatima—1917-1967*, which presents a critical view of the apparitions. The paper, devoted to Fatima, is well edited.

Daughters of St. Paul (50 St. Paul's Ave., Boston, MA 02130).
"*Fatima, Cove of Wonders*" 300 pp. Cloth, $4.50, paper, $3.25; "*Fatima, Hope of the World*" half-hour documentary movie; "*Our Lady of Fatima*" drama, feature movie, 16 mm. Movies are for rent or for sale. The book is by Alphonse M. Cappa, S.S.P.

Fatima From the Beginning Fr. De Marchi, I.M.C.
This is a later edition of Fr. John De Marchi's 1950 work. It has valuable additions, including papal documents and an excerpt from Pope John Paul II's homily at Fatima, May 13,

1982. Available from Consolata Missions, Fatima, Portugal (in English).

Videntes da Fatima This eight-page bulletin is published in English as *The Seers of Fatima* by Fr. Luis Kondor, S.V.D., the vice-postulator for Francisco and Jacinta. (Rua S. Pedro 9, Apart 6, P 2496 Fatima Codex, Portugal). It will keep you up-to-date on the progress of their separate causes.

ROBERT J. NESNICK
Casa de Jacinta Marto
Moita-Rodondo
Cova Da Iria, Portugal

Robert Nesnick is an American veteran who worked for a time in the U.S. for social causes. When he went to Fatima, he believed that he had discovered a cause that would bring greater benefits, and more lasting good to people. He bought a house at Fatima in which he lives and which is his workshop for promoting Francisco, Jacinta and St. Therese, the Little Flower. He has distributed pieces of literature in the tens of thousands. In the past few years, he has taken hundreds of pictures of places associated with the children, and is making investigations of details associated with them. His favorite, as we may judge by the name of his house, is Jacinta.